# outbreak

*Plagues That Changed History*

Written and Illustrated by
**BRYN BARNARD**

Crown Publishers ♛ New York

# The Invisible Hand
## How microbes shape civilization

## Invaders within

You're born pristine and alone, but it doesn't last. With your first independent breath, your body becomes a cooperative venture with other creatures: a colony, a host. You become infected.

The creatures that invade your body are called *microbes*. Invisible to the eye, so small they have to be measured in millionths of a meter, these tiny organisms are mostly single-celled bacteria. They arrive via the air you breathe, the water you drink, the surfaces you touch, and the food you eat. They colonize your skin, your hair, your mouth, your eyes, your ears, and your intestines. By the time you're an adult, you'll be carrying around about two pounds of these creatures, mostly in your gut. In sheer numbers, they'll make up 95 percent of all the cells in your body, about ten quadrillion in all.

This is a good thing. These microbes are *symbionts*. Our survival depends on cooperative coexistence with them. Symbionts exist with us in a mutually beneficial relationship. We give them protection and nourishment. They keep our bodily ecology in balance. Outside, symbionts keep our skin tidy, our eyelashes groomed, our armpits from rotting. Inside, symbionts help digest food, produce essential vitamins, and protect us from disease. We couldn't stay healthy without them.

## Lifestyles of the small and deadly

Many microbes are not symbionts. Some are free-living creatures like us. They putter around the soil, the forest floor, the oceans and streams, our kitchen countertops and toilets. Others inhabit environments too extreme for most other living things: polar wastes, volcanic vents, nuclear reactors, chemical soups. They live, reproduce, and die on their own, doing us no harm.

The majority of microbes, however, are neither helpful nor benign, neither symbiotic nor free-living. They are parasites. They live in us or on us at our expense. The original parasites were people and the term wasn't an insult. In ancient Greece, parasites were religious workers who served at temple feasts

(*parasite* means "beside food"). Over the centuries, however, the term changed to describe a professional dinner guest who flattered or amused the host. Eventually *parasite* came to mean any creature who takes without giving. In the case of microbial parasites, *we* are the feasts. Sometimes they only steal a little of our food or energy. Sometimes they alter our lifestyle to ensure their survival. Sometimes they make us get sick or die. Microbial parasites include both bacteria and more complex one-celled creatures called protozoans, plus multicelled worms and flukes. They also include viruses, vanishingly small creatures that are neither living nor dead. Viruses invade our bodies and replicate, using our cells as fuel and housing.

All these parasitic microbes are the unseen part of a much larger visible parasitic world that includes mosquitoes, ticks, leeches, and many kinds of worms. Parasitism, it turns out, is an astonishingly popular lifestyle. There are four times as many kinds of parasites on earth as free-livers. Most free-living organisms host several parasites. Many parasites host other parasites. And some of those parasites have parasites of their own. They divide and subdivide the delectable, concentrated food supply of their hosts into precisely defined real estate and fiercely defended turf.

## Sick society

Microbial parasites can change not just individuals but entire societies. If enough people live closely together and other conditions are right, an infectious microbe—a *pathogen*—can spread widely through a population. These are called *epidemics* and are as old as civilization. One famous Chinese catalog of epidemics lists some 304, starting in 243 B.C. and ending in A.D. 1911. Some epidemics race through populations like summer brush fires, consuming all they touch in a few months, then burning themselves out and disappearing until another season. Others move like glaciers, carving their way through a population over decades. If the disease is particularly successful, becoming continental or global in scope, it's called a *pandemic*. If the pathogen settles in and becomes a permanent feature of a region, it is known as *endemic*.

But whether fast or slow, epidemic, pandemic, or

*Antoni van Leeuwenhoek was the first person to see and describe bacteria.*

endemic, these infectious diseases can force enormous, sometimes cataclysmic changes on societies. They can reshuffle power, serve the greater good, or solidify the status of the ruling class. They can determine not just who lives and who dies, but who wins and who loses, who gets wealthy and who stays poor, which ideas become popular and which ones wither away. Without epidemics, ours would be a very different world indeed.

*Outbreak* is the story of epidemics that have transformed human society. Of the thousands of epidemics that have occurred across human history, this book focuses on six of the most extraordinary: bubonic plague, smallpox, tuberculosis, cholera, yellow fever, and influenza. (Other epidemics, like AIDS, are supporting cast members.) Each chapter describes the origin of the pathogen, its spread, its treatment and cures, and its most influential outbreak. Many of these pathogens have been some of the most feared killers on the planet. Some still are. All have been crucial in changing the way we think and act.

## The truth is tiny

Looking at how diseases have changed society tells us a lot about how science has evolved, too. Humanity's understanding of the role of microbes in the spread of illness has been a slow, halting, convoluted journey of discovery. Along the way we've taken many wrong turns, traveled up many box canyons, been led down many blind alleys.

It took thousands of men and women working over many centuries to uncover the simple truths about infection we take for granted today. Of the many important names in the history of epidemics, a few stand out. First in line is an Italian physician, Girolamo Fracastoro, who in the early 1500s guessed that tiny, unseen *seminaria contagium* (seeds of contagion) might spread disease. More famous is the Dutch cloth merchant and amateur lens grinder Antoni van Leeuwenhoek. In 1674, with his own homemade microscope, he became the first person to see and describe microbes, the first person to truly comprehend the existence of this previously invisible world. He called these new creatures *animalcules*. But he did not link them to disease.

Two centuries after Leeuwenhoek, people still didn't think microbes caused sickness. They knew microbes existed. They knew they were present on wounds and other injury sites. But microbes were perceived as a by-product of illness. By 1865, French chemist Louis Pasteur had made the critical breakthrough: he proved that microbes actually *cause* infection. He called them *germs*. Pasteur's "germ theory of disease" opened the doors to understanding how illnesses are contracted and spread. His method of killing pathogens with heat—*pasteurization*—is still used to make many foods safe to consume. By 1884, Pasteur's German rival, Robert Koch, had developed a method for testing the microbe-disease connection. His Koch Postulates are still the gold standard for determining whether a microbe causes illness.

Over the decades that followed, the competition between Koch, Pasteur, their students, and their rivals unraveled the mysteries of one infectious disease after another. The thresholds these explorers crossed made it possible for their successors to produce today's medical miracles: antibiotics and vaccines, organ transplants and gene therapy, low infant mortality and high population growth. Slowly, scientist by scientist, revelation by revelation, the veil was lifted and our perception of pathogens changed. Looking for the invisible hand guiding our destiny? You can track it in the economy, find it in holy scripture, or sense it in the grand sweep of the stars. But there's another truth, a different truth, a smaller truth. It's closer than you think. Just look in a microscope.

# Smithereens
## How the Black Death smashed feudal Europe

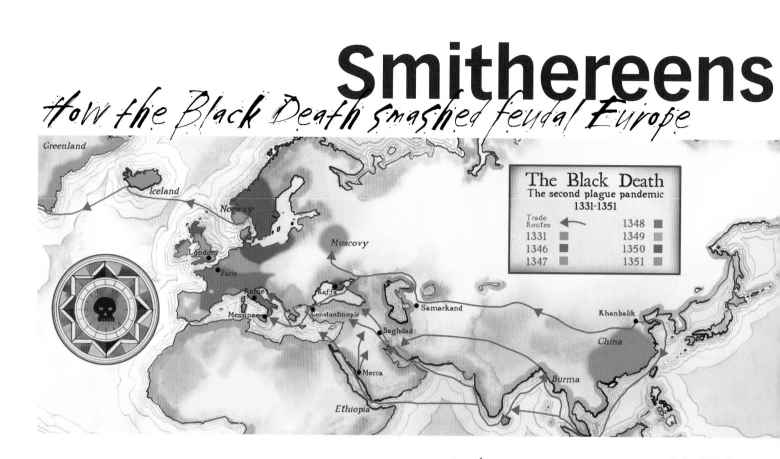

The Black Death
The second plague pandemic
1331-1351

| Trade Routes | ← | | |
| --- | --- | --- | --- |
| 1331 | | 1348 | |
| 1346 | | 1349 | |
| 1347 | | 1350 | |
| | | 1351 | |

## End times

Great epidemics, like wars, natural disasters, and other catastrophes, can expose the fragility of human society. Given enough stress, what seems the most solid and immobile social system can shatter. Such was the case in fourteenth-century Europe, a frozen society built on vast inequality and limited social mobility. For nearly a thousand years, Europeans were held in the rigid, unyielding grip of two interconnected forces: the feudal aristocracy and the Catholic Church. A third group, the knights, enforced their will. These power centers controlled all the wealth, owned all the land, determined all the laws, and were gatekeepers of all knowledge. They ruled over a body of ill-paid, ill-housed, illiterate peasant serfs, who did the work. Compared to competing regions like the inquisitive and inventive realm of golden age Islam or the continent-spanning empire of the Mongols, Europe was a Podunk backwater.

The arrival in 1346 of a new disease changed this situation. Arcing across Europe from the Mediterranean to Scandinavia, the epidemic caused victims to become feverish and grow painful black welts that exuded a nauseating stench. Half who were sickened by the illness died. Europeans called it the Great Mortality, the Pestilence, and the Pest. We call it the Black Death. In four years, it destroyed a third of Europe's population. Afterward, nothing in Europe was quite the same. The entire structure of European society became more porous, more mobile. With fewer workers, wages went up. With fewer consumers, prices went down. In both the countryside and the cities, a rising middle class was able to accumulate, at bargain prices, the land, businesses, and wealth the dead had left behind. This economic revolution in turn sparked other changes: in law (to make sense of the new order), in the arts (to reflect on the horror and show off the new money), and in trade (to accumulate even more). In the Church, the catastrophe smashed an ossified orthodoxy, leading to questions, inventions, heresy, wars, and ultimately a world with not one Christianity but many. Finally, in the world of the nobility, the social, economic, and political crises caused by the Black Death were blows from which the ruling classes never fully recovered. Bit by bit, their power seeped away to others, never to return.

## Keep the faith

Even before the arrival of the Black Death, Europe was heading for a brick wall of trouble. By the beginning of the fourteenth century, the population had grown to an unprecedented seventy-three million. Cities were crowded and filthy, filled with people who hardly ever bathed. Sewerage was inadequate, so rotting garbage and human waste were heaped in streets or dumped in rivers. Moreover, around 1280, the climate had begun cooling. Summers became shorter, winters harsher, and harvests worse. Nearly all the forests had been cut down. No more farmland

4

To protect themselves from the Black Death, physicians wore a special outfit: a waxed-linen robe, a wide-brimmed hat, gloves, and a mask that featured glass lenses and a long beak filled with vinegar-soaked cloth and spices to counteract the stench of dying patients. Their preferred way of trying to cure patients was by bleeding them.

was available. People began to starve. Pessimism and persecution grew.

Adaptation to changing conditions was difficult, for the Church discouraged innovation and independent ideas. Priests enforced unswerving loyalty to the Pope and belief in orthodox Christian dogma. This included the conviction that we were born with original sin and lived cursed. Illness, like all of life's troubles, was the result of sin. Christians dared not waver from these teachings. They risked excommunication or worse.

Medical knowledge had also stalled. Since 1300, Pope Boniface VIII had forbidden the dissection of human cadavers (pigs were used instead). Human anatomy remained a mystery. The function of many organs, even the circulation of the blood, was unknown. Physicians continued to depend on the thousand-year-old teachings of the fifth-century-B.C. Greek physician Hippocrates and his second-century-A.D. Roman follower Galen. These two influential doctors believed that illness was caused by an imbalance in bodily "humors." An excess of hot blood, for example, was thought to cause fever. It was curable by phlebotomy: bloodletting. This approach to human health would prove utterly useless in combating the plague. Physicians did their best with the tools at their disposal, but for the most part they could only watch helplessly as their patients died.

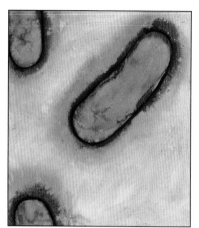
*The bacterium* Yersinia pestis

## Germ warfare

The Black Death probably started in 1331 in Central Asia, carried there by infected Mongol troops returning from Burma. By 1346, having killed millions and traveled with armies and traders along the Silk Road, the epidemic arrived on the Black Sea's Crimean Peninsula. There a Tartar army was besieging the city of Kaffa. To break the city's defenses, the attackers catapulted diseased corpses over the walls. Genoese merchants trading there fled via ship to Messina, Sicily. Sick and dying, they arrived in October 1347, bringing plague to the Italian peninsula.

Nearly everywhere the plague reached, victims died faster than they could be buried. In Pisa, five hundred people a day died. In Paris, eight hundred a day died. In Vienna, six hundred a day died. In Avignon, when the graveyards were filled, corpses were dumped

in the Rhône River. In Bordeaux, rotting cadavers were stacked on the docks and in the streets. By December 1348, the epidemic arrived in England. Bodies there overflowed mass graves. It soon spread to Norway, Sweden, Denmark, Prussia, Iceland, and even distant Greenland. In 1351, when the epidemic seemed to be finally over, officials of Pope Clement VI estimated that 23,840,000 people were gone. Nearly a third of Europe's population had been killed by the disease.

## Deadly diseases for $100

What was the Black Death? The most common explanation for the epidemic is bubonic plague, a disease passed to people by rodents. Historically, plague had been confined to populations of rats in isolated mountain regions, one in South Asia and the other in East Africa. When human activities like war and trade disturbed these ancient reservoirs, the plague escaped its natural confines. The devastating Justinian's Plague that hit the Mediterranean in A.D. 542 was likely bubonic, imported by Roman soldiers returning from Ethiopia. The Roman Empire never recovered, and European power shifted north; a century later, Islam became the predominant civilization of the eastern Mediterranean. The World Health Organization calls this the first plague pandemic. The Black Death was the beginning of the second. In all, that second pandemic lasted over three hundred years. Plague returned several times in the 1500s, struck London in the Great Plague of 1664–66, and finally sputtered out in the 1750s.

Plague is caused by a bacterium called *Yersinia pestis*, named after the student of Pasteur who discovered it in 1894, Alexander Yersin. This microbe is a parasite that lives in fleas that live on rodents. These animals—fleas and rodents—are *vectors* (transmitters) of the disease. If an infected flea jumps from a rodent host and bites a person, it injects thousands of plague bacteria into the wound. They travel through the body's lymph system to nodes in the groin and armpits, excreting toxins that kill human cells. As the body's immune system tries to destroy the invaders, the skin blackens and the nodes swell into the disease's characteristic buboes (from the Greek *boubon*, "groin," thus the term "bubonic plague"). This isn't the worst of it. Victims get feverish and suffer from vomiting, bouts of diarrhea, and respiratory distress before recovering or dying. If the bacteria migrate to the lungs (pneumonic plague), death is virtually certain. A victim who breathes in *Yersinia pestis* from a bacteria-loaded cough can die within hours.

## Better them than us, m'lord

Europeans who experienced the Black Death had no idea what caused the disease, but they had some inventive guesses. Some people blamed *miasmas*, poisonous gases they believed were released from the ground by, among other things, earthquakes. To ward off miasmas, they would barricade themselves in their houses (Pope Clement VI did this) or flee to the countryside. Other people thought the Pest was caused by the malevolent influence of the planets. Astrology was taken very seriously in those days. Saturn, Jupiter, and Mars had been aligned in the House of Aquarius, a bad sign. Not blamed were the legions of rats that fed on the omnipresent filth, or the fleas that tormented everyone. Like the wretched odors, they were just part of life's daily struggles.

In an attempt to slow the spread of the disease, city officials in Venice instituted the *quaranta giorni* (from which we get the word *quarantine*), named after the period Jesus spent in the wilderness. It was a forty-day period of isolation for newly arrived ships, to ensure that any onboard epidemic would burn itself out before the passengers were allowed to mingle with the general population. To treat the disease, doctors bled patients and also lanced and drained buboes to relieve pain. Priests ministered to the sick with prayer.

No one knew when the mass dying would stop. Some Christians were convinced this was the long-awaited end times, the apocalypse prophesied in the Bible's Book of Revelation that would accompany the Second Coming of Christ. Other people became unhinged. They partied wildly or even robbed and murdered. In Germany, increasing numbers of people joined the Flagellants. Adherents of this popular sect sought God's forgiveness by whipping themselves bloody with iron-tipped lashes. By 1350, the movement had been stamped out by order of the Pope, but not before the Flagellants had turned blame for the plague on the Jews, Europe's perennial scapegoat of choice. They were accused of causing the plague by poisoning Europe's wells.

Jews were rightless noncitizens, serfs of the king, continually degraded and persecuted for refusing to convert to Christianity. Thomas Aquinas called them "slaves of the Church." In 1205, Pope Innocent III had damned them to perpetual servitude for their role in the death of Jesus. But Jews were also essential cogs in Christendom's economy. They were banned from most occupations but allowed to lend money at interest (Christians were forbidden this job). They were heavily taxed, so interest rates were high. Thus, they made handy tools for extracting wealth from the population and useful social lightning rods, diverting civil unrest away from the rulers.

In those days, it didn't take much to incite a Christian mob to attack Jews. Across Europe they did

so nearly every year during Easter week. Killings at other times were not infrequent. But the plague massacres were larger and more terrible then anything European Jewry had ever experienced. In 1348 and 1349, Christian Europeans tried, tortured, burned, murdered, and executed Jews by the thousands. Many leaders, including Pope Clement VI, condemned these acts. But other notables, who had borrowed heavily from Jewish moneylenders, effectively canceled those debts by instigating or leading the attacks. After the plague, confiscated Jewish property was the basis for several Gentile fortunes. Such thefts are only one example of the way the plague turned society on its head.

## Swept away

The feudal order died with the plague and the system that would become capitalism was born. With fewer hands available, the lot of peasants improved. No longer tied to a particular estate, they could work where they pleased, where wages were highest. Outraged rulers tried repressing raises with wage laws, but employers, desperate for workers, ignored them. When the authorities tried to crack down, peasants revolted. In England, they nearly brought down the government.

With more money, peasants could eat better, use silverware, afford nicer clothes, and move into upscale housing. For many, these changes would be temporary.

Soon enough, they were poor again. But for some—particularly merchants, traders, and bankers—the postplague chaos offered numerous opportunities to move up in the world. For the quick, the opportunistic, and the ruthless, wealth that previously had taken generations to acquire could be amassed in a few years. Among this increasingly influential class of people, status and power was measured not in land, titles, and familial connections, but in money.

As the lot of merchants improved, nobles' fortunes declined. Many noble families were immiserated or exterminated by the plague. Inheritance claims were chaotic. Disputes over who really owned what provided years of employment for lawyers. From these battles evolved a confusing welter of real estate laws and the take-no-prisoners style of lawsuits still with us today.

As economic distinctions blurred, social distinctions sharpened. To show off their status, nobles dressed more extravagantly. At the same time, they enacted "sumptuary laws" that specified what types of clothing could be worn by commoners, to prevent the newly wealthy from dressing or eating like their betters. Nobles also treated the new rich with contempt. But, like it or not, the merchant class was here to stay. Eventually they would outshine the nobility. With every century, as global trade and urbanization increased, financiers, bankers, and traders became more and more dominant. In time—our

*The Flagellants were a popular religious movement that spread across Central Europe during the Black Death. Flagellants traveled in groups from town to town, led by a Master to whom they swore allegiance. They wore distinctive hooded costumes and sought God's forgiveness by beating themselves bloody with iron-tipped whips.*

time—they would become more powerful than most governments.

## Thanks be to plague

Neither the Church nor medical science could offer satisfactory answers to the plague. The sinful and the pious had died in equal numbers. Among the dead were three successive archbishops of Canterbury, seven of the Pope's cardinals, and many, many priests. With such a massive die-off, the Church's power was severely eroded. Its monopoly on knowledge was broken. Latin, the language of the Church, began a long decline. Vernacular writing (English, French, German, and Italian) flourished. So did a pessimistic style of art that emphasized death, decay, sin, and the torments of hell. New religious ideas spread, eventually leading to the Protestant Reformation and the rational thinking of the Enlightenment. For some, this would include the denial of God altogether.

Even Catholicism eventually changed. In 1348, Pope Clement VI lifted the ban on human dissection, so doctors could try to understand what caused the Black Death. The age of modern medicine starts here. In 1965, the Church finally (and officially) stopped blaming all Jews for the death of Jesus. It was a belated admission, six hundred years after the Black Death, that the need for a feudal scapegoat, like feudalism itself, had vanished. Capitalism, and the mobile, porous, dynamic society it powers, was here to stay.

While the cultural, economic, political, and scientific changes wrought by the Black Death continue to resonate down the centuries to the present day, plague itself hasn't gone away. The third plague pandemic started in Hong Kong in 1894 and has yet to end. Initially, shipboard rats spread plague to rodent reservoirs around the world, from marmots in Siberia to squirrels and prairie dogs in the Americas. So far, the third pandemic has killed about thirteen million people, most in the early twentieth century. The pandemic is being controlled, but only with vigilance and fast action. Eradicating diseased rodents can control outbreaks, and victims can be successfully treated with antibiotics. A 1994 epidemic in India was stopped this way.

In 1995, however, a plague strain showed up in Madagascar that is resistant to all known antibiotics. In 2004, plague broke out among the desert gerbils of Turkmenistan, a country with no functioning health system and a dictator who has fired all foreign-trained doctors. Because the country's government-controlled press is forbidden to mention the disease, it is uncertain how many people are affected or dead. It remains to be seen whether this outbreak will be controlled or spread.

So a global Black Death and all that might mean for humanity is a remote nightmare. But it's not impossible.

# Empires of Infection
## How smallpox conquered the world

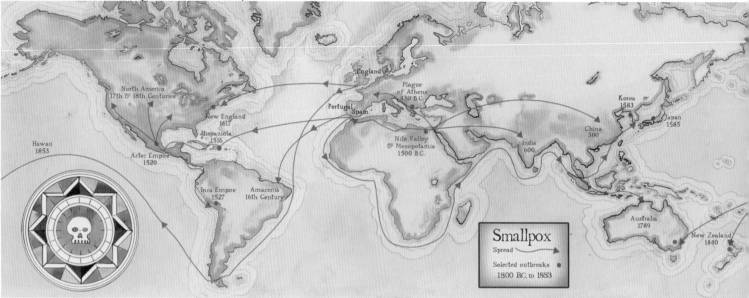

North America
17th & 18th Centuries

New England
1617

Hispaniola
1516

Hawaii
1853

Aztec Empire
1520

Inca Empire
1527

Amazonia
16th Century

England

Plague
of Athens
430 B.C.

Portugal
Spain

Nile Valley
& Mesopotamia
1500 B.C.

India
600

China
300

Korea
1583

Japan
1585

Australia
1789

New Zealand
1840

**Smallpox**

Spread

Selected outbreaks
1500 B.C. to 1853

## A busy year

The year 1492 closed one door for Spain and opened another for the world. In January, the armies of King Ferdinand and Queen Isabella toppled Granada, the last Muslim stronghold in their Christian kingdom. In March, they published the Edict of Expulsion, which required all Jews to either convert to Christianity or depart within three months, leaving property and precious metal behind. These two events effectively ended Spain's golden age of religious tolerance and intellectual brilliance, the *convivencia* (coexistence), a period of Christian, Jewish, and Muslim amity. Indeed, Sultan Beyazit II of Turkey is said to have remarked of the Jews pouring into his realm, "How can anyone call Ferdinand wise when he impoverishes his kingdom to enrich mine?" In August, another of the king and queen's projects got under way: Christopher Columbus set sail on his intrepid voyage to the Indies. For this gamble, Columbus demanded the title Admiral of the Oceans, a coat of arms, and 10 percent of the profits. His promises of gold, slaves, converts to Christianity, and new land across the sea marked the beginning of the Spanish Empire, the start of European dominance, and the globalization of disease.

Although many explorers from other societies preceded Columbus, 1492 is the starting gate of the Age of Exploration because it caused permanent European colonization and long-lasting worldwide change. It ignited an unprecedented race for discovery and empire. It opened the transatlantic slave trade (Columbus was a champion slaver, exporting more human beings from America than any other single individual). It exposed Europe to new political ideas and a bulging cornucopia of New World foods. Most importantly, it unleashed the greatest biological assault in history.

## Tiny warriors

Columbus and the Europeans who rushed after him had a few advantages over Native Americans, including oceangoing ships, advanced navigation, deadly firearms, and an implacable belief in the superiority of their culture and religion. These alone, however, were not enough to ensure Europe's conquest of the New World. The Native Americans were many, after all, and the first Europeans few. The explorers often arrived sick and hungry. They were dependent on native hospitality for survival. Once the natives understood that the Europeans intended to enslave them and steal their land, they resisted fiercely. In a fair fight, they often won.

Europe's decisive (albeit unwitting) advantage was disease. The explorers brimmed with pathogens to which the Native Americans had no immunity: hepatitis, influenza, typhus, typhoid, diphtheria, measles, mumps, and smallpox. The arrival of the Europeans was like the detonation of a biological bomb. In two generations, the majority of Americans (population

Smallpox raced across North America, depopulating the continent ahead of European colonists. In the Pacific Northwest, the Native American villages of Puget Sound were emptied of inhabitants well before George Vancouver arrived to explore the land for England.

guesstimates range from ten to one hundred million) were dead. In two centuries, their cultures had been almost completely replaced by "neo-Europes"—not just European people and European culture, but European clover and honeybees, crops and weeds, cattle, horses, dogs, cats, and birds. Later, the same phenomenon was accomplished in Australia and New Zealand.

Of all the diseases Europeans introduced to the Americas and other new worlds, smallpox had the most devastating impact, killing more Native Americans than any other illness. Smallpox attacks the skin, internal organs, throat, and eyes. It causes a fever, headache, rash, and masses of painful, pus-filled bumps called pustules. From 30 to 90 percent of those who get smallpox die. For hosts who survive, the pustules scab over and fall off, leaving deeply pitted scars, possible blindness, and lifelong immunity to the virus.

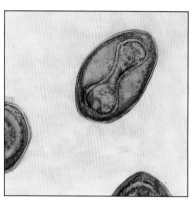
*The variola virus*

Smallpox was the decisive factor in the Spanish conquest of Mexico and Peru and the Portuguese invasion of Brazil, sowing confusion and terror among the defenders and reducing their numerical superiority. Later, smallpox swept across North America ahead of French and British colonists, emptying the land for occupation by the invaders. Given the terrible nature of the illness and the high mortality, it is remarkable Native Americans were able to offer any resistance at all.

Smallpox is believed to have originated in Africa thousands of years ago. The first recorded instance was during a war between the Egyptians and the Hittites in 1350 B.C. It spread from there to Persia, India, and China. Both the Indians and the Chinese worshiped their own versions of a smallpox goddess, to whom they prayed for deliverance. Europe's first contact with smallpox may have been Greece's devastating Plague of Athens, which appeared in 430 B.C. It killed the great orator Pericles and brought down the Athenian Empire. Continental smallpox epidemics did not appear until the Crusades in the tenth to fourteenth centuries, when thousands of European warriors inadvertently brought smallpox back from their invasions of the Middle East. By the time of Columbus's voyage, smallpox was endemic in Europe. An epidemic in Paris in 1438 killed 50,000 people, mostly children.

### Paradise lost

After Columbus arrived on the Caribbean island of Hispaniola, his reports back to Europe suggested paradise. The island's Taino inhabitants had no monarchy and little hierarchy, a concept that flabbergasted Europeans. (Philosopher John Locke would later write, "In the beginning, all the world was America.") The Spanish set to work to destroy this Eden. They forced the Taino to serve as beasts of burden. They took their food. They made them search for gold. They shot them for sport. Finally, they fed the corpses to their dogs. By 1516, when smallpox first appeared on Hispaniola, Spanish cruelty had reduced the indigenous population from an estimated two million to eight million to a mere 12,000. Smallpox finished the job. In 1510, the Spanish began importing African slave replacements. By 1555, the Taino were nearly extinct.

The Taino, like other Native Americans, had no immunity to European disease for several reasons. First, they were descended from Siberian immigrants. Thousands of years before, the ancestors of most Native Americans had walked across the frozen Bering Strait through the Arctic's frigid decontamination zone. Pathogens accustomed to balmier climes couldn't survive the journey and were left behind. Second, unlike Europeans, Native Americans didn't keep much livestock. Domesticated animals are the source of many lethal human illnesses, including tuberculosis, influenza, measles, and smallpox. The Native Americans had neither many animal candidates for domestication, nor a useful version of the wheel to put them to work. Finally, the Americans had far better hygiene than the Europeans. They bathed regularly and kept their villages and cities clean, reducing contact with potential pathogens. They were tall, healthy, long-lived, and utterly defenseless.

One of the most infamous smallpox episodes occurred during the Spanish conquest of Mexico. In 1519, Hernán Cortés led a band of 550 conquistadors from Cuba to the Mexican mainland. Their goal was Tenochtitlán, capital of the Aztec Empire, a city rumored to be awash in gold. Cortés's group reached the city in November. The emperor, Montezuma, welcomed the Spanish as descendants of the Aztec god Quetzalcoatl. In return, Cortés captured Montezuma, ransomed him for gold, then tried to rule the Aztecs through him. By this time (the spring of 1520), a rival Spanish expedition led by Pánfilo de

*During Hernán Cortés's conquest of the Aztec capital, Tenochtitlán, smallpox killed a quarter of the capital's population within a few weeks. Although many of the demoralized survivors abandoned their gods and embraced Christianity, they continued dying from the disease.*

Narváez had arrived in Mexico. One of Narváez's crew had smallpox. Cortés left the capital to repel this rival. In the battle between the two invaders, one of Cortés's soldiers became infected.

The Aztecs, who outnumbered the Spanish a hundred to one, revolted during Cortés's absence and defeated him upon his return. The Spanish fled for their lives. During the fighting, however, at least one of the Aztecs caught smallpox from the Spanish. A devastating epidemic broke out among the natives. Within a few weeks, a quarter of the capital's population was dead, including Montezuma and much of the army. The corpses littered the ground "like bedbugs." When Cortés regrouped and returned, the Spanish easily beat the demoralized survivors. The Aztec Empire was finished.

"Virgin soil" epidemics like this occurred wherever the Europeans set foot in the Americas. By 1527, the disease had spread south to the Inca Empire, killing the emperor and about 100,000 of his subjects. The epidemic sparked a civil war that had barely ended in 1532 when Spanish conquistador Francisco Pizarro arrived with about six hundred men. They captured the new emperor, Atahuallpa, ransomed him for a roomful of gold, then killed him. By chance, they also imported a second smallpox epidemic that killed so many Incans that fields were left uncultivated. Still more people died of famine. By the end of the six-

teenth century, three-quarters of the Incans were dead. Meanwhile, in Brazil, the Portuguese were introducing the natives of the Amazon to Christianity and smallpox. The Indians died by the tens of thousands. Across the Americas, conqueror and conquered agreed that God was on the side of the invulnerable Europeans. It perplexed religious leaders, however, that though terrified natives converted to Christianity in droves, smallpox kept killing them.

## The Blessed Pox

Smallpox was essential to the English and French conquest of North America. In 1617, three years before the arrival of the Pilgrims at Plymouth, a virgin soil epidemic passed through what would become New England, killing 90 to 94 percent of the inhabitants. The Pilgrims found a nearly empty land of abandoned villages and fields covered with the bones of the dead. Smallpox returned again and again, making the first fifty years of British colonization a virtual cakewalk: they could take what they wanted with little resistance. No wonder King George III called the disease "the Blessed Pox." Smallpox moved westward across the continent ahead of the pioneers in a great wave of death.

These epidemics were not always accidental. In 1763, during the final years of the French and Indian Wars, General Jeffrey Amherst, commander of the

British forces, recommended a gift of smallpox-laced blankets to jumpstart an epidemic among Native Americans. His goal was genocide, or as he put it, to "…Extirpate this Execrable Race." This is only the most notorious instance of British and American biological warfare against the natives.

By the time English explorer George Vancouver cruised Puget Sound in 1792, the villages there were deserted, the beaches littered with skeletons. Smallpox had crossed the continent ahead of him.

## Not so blessed

Unlike the plague bacterium, smallpox is a virus that has no host other than humans. An epidemic can only spread from person to person. In the densely populated cities of Europe, smallpox moved through the population at a pace that ensured someone was always infected, so that each new generation of susceptible babies got exposed. In this continuous "chain of infection," one got the disease, passed it on, and survived or died. Most city folk who made it to adulthood were invulnerable to smallpox outbreaks for the rest of their lives.

After the first generation of colonists established themselves in the New World, smallpox became nearly as bad a problem for their children as it was for the natives they were trying to exterminate. America's colonial settlements were sparsely populated. Once smallpox had burned through all the susceptible people in a rural community, the chain of infection was broken. Smallpox could vanish completely for a generation. Only after enough vulnerable new hosts were born would a chance encounter with an infected individual start another epidemic. Between 1636 and 1717, Boston suffered seven separate smallpox epidemics.

Europeans tried the usual unproductive methods to stop smallpox—bleeding, enemas, purgatives, and prayer. They also used quarantine to some effect. But Asia and Africa already had a preventative that worked. For centuries, the Chinese had been using inoculation: deliberate infection with smallpox to create a mild form of the illness. In the Chinese procedure, smallpox scabs were ground into powder and blown up a person's nose. Indians, Africans, and Turks used another variant: injecting scab power or smallpox pus directly into a wound in the skin. Either way, the patient would get sick, recover, and be immune for life. Inoculation had disadvantages: once inoculated, a person was fully infectious and could get others sick.

Worse, one in fifty would die—not great odds, but better than those of an actual epidemic.

## Who wants to be first?

Inoculation was also called variolization, from *variola*, the official European term for smallpox. *Variola* was derived from the Latin *varius* ("spotted") or *varus* ("pimple"). It came to be called "the small pox" to distinguish the disease from the symptoms of "the great pox," a very different illness that appeared in Europe soon after Columbus returned from the New World. We call that disease syphilis.

Effective European efforts to prevent smallpox started in 1717 when Lady Mary Wortley Montagu, a smallpox survivor, learned about inoculation in Turkey. She called the procedure ingrafting. Later, it came to be called variolization. In 1718, Montagu had

*Variolization was practiced for centuries in the Far East, the Middle East, and Africa before the Europeans adopted the technique to immunize people against smallpox. In the Chinese version, dried smallpox scabs were blown up a patient's nose, causing a mild case of the illness. People so treated had a one-in-fifty chance of dying. Survivors were immune for life.*

her son inoculated. In 1721, she returned to England and had her daughter inoculated. They survived and were proved immune. But British leaders resisted. Male doctors scoffed at a woman's medical suggestion. Religious officials worried that without disease as a whip, people wouldn't fear God. It took successful experimentation on prisoners and orphans and acceptance by Montagu's friends in the British royal family to popularize inoculation. Meanwhile, on the other side of the Atlantic, Reverend Cotton Mather learned about the African version of the procedure from his slave Onesimus. Mather introduced variolization to Boston. By the Revolutionary War, George Washington would inoculate the entire Continental army.

The epochal year in smallpox prevention, however, was 1796, when British doctor Edward Jenner proved that inoculation with the harmless *vaccina* (cowpox) virus prevented infection with smallpox. He called this procedure vaccination. His discovery was published in a pamphlet that was translated into German, French, Spanish, Dutch, Italian, and Latin. Vaccination quickly spread around the world, but it took nearly two more centuries to wipe out the disease. By 1977, a heroic decades-long campaign of global vaccination by the World Health Organization finally broke the last link in the smallpox infection chain. Smallpox was eradicated from the wild. The virus still exists, though it is confined to a freezer. Two, actually: one in the United States, the other in Russia.

# The Cost of Doing Business
### How yellow fever stopped slavery

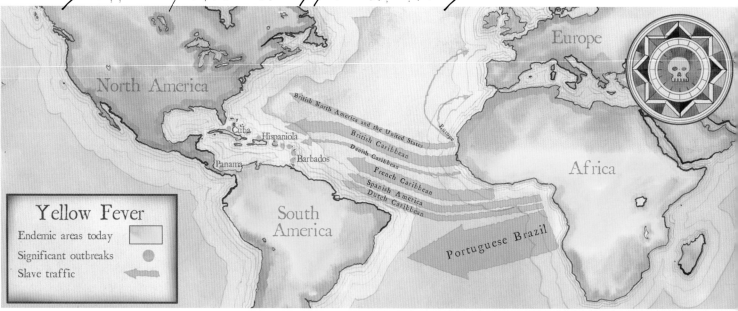

## Too good to be true

Survivors of certain infectious diseases are invulnerable to repeat epidemics. This immunity gives them the ultimate advantage. When the illness returns, they will remain healthy while others sicken and die. This difference between the immune and susceptible has sometimes had historically significant consequences. In the case of yellow fever, the significance was truly awesome: it helped bring an end to New World slavery.

In the sixteenth century, Europe had conquered the Aztecs, the Incas, and the indigenous people of the Caribbean and much of Amazonia and eastern North America. The New World seemed an inexhaustible supply of wealth: land for the taking, gold and silver from its mines, food from its farms, hides, feathers, pelts, wood, and dyes from its forests. Most importantly, the New World was an astonishingly fertile place to plant a valuable Old World crop: sugar. Sugar plantations needed a source of plentiful, cheap workers—preferably slaves. Europe itself wouldn't do; the continent was still underpopulated from the Black Death. With demand for labor exceeding supply, peasants had power: wages were going up. Nor was the New World a potential slave-labor pool, for European depredation and disease had nearly wiped out the Native American population.

The obvious alternative was Africa, a continent European explorers and colonists were just beginning to exploit. Africa already had a bustling slave trade to satisfy local and Muslim demand. The Europeans simply redirected the flow across the Atlantic and opened the spigot full blast. The deadly irony of this choice would become apparent too late. Along with the estimated twenty million Africans enslaved and shipped to America for European greed came yellow fever, an African disease to which most slaves were immune but slave owners were not. The illness would prove to be slavery's undoing, first in the Caribbean, then in North and South America. Later, the disease would also play an important role in the United States' efforts to project its power throughout the region.

## Welcome home

Human beings have lived in Africa longer than on any other continent. Pathogens that live there too have become exquisitely adapted to exploiting us. Malaria, yellow fever, river blindness, and elephantiasis are just a few of the diseases that coevolved with people, fine-tuning their life cycles to our own. Thousands of years ago, when many of our ancestors left Africa to populate temperate regions, they managed to leave many of these parasites behind. But when Europeans returned to conquer Africa, the microbes were waiting. In West Africa, tropical diseases killed so many Europeans the region was nicknamed "the white man's grave." Within a year of arrival, most would-be conquerors weren't running plantations or sipping gin on the veranda, they were composting in

Yellow fever would often break out on slave ships at sea, sickening and killing the European crew. Adult Africans who had survived the disease as children were immune, a black invulnerability whites found mystifying.

the soil. The image of the European explorer or missionary dying in his tent from some tropical illness was so common it became a literary cliché. "Beware, beware the Bight of Benin," warned one British rhyme about West Africa. "One comes out where fifty went in."

Yellow fever proved an exceptionally portable African disease. On ships leaving Africa for the New World, the fever would usually strike a week or so into the voyage. Mild cases would feel like the flu: the symptoms would pass and the host would recover. In severe cases, however, the illness would progress from fever, blinding headaches, chills, and intense muscle pain to bleeding from the nose and mouth. Blood would collect in the stomach, coagulate and darken, and exit as yellow fever's unmistakable black vomit. Eventually the liver would fail, turning the skin a jaundiced yellow. Death would follow.

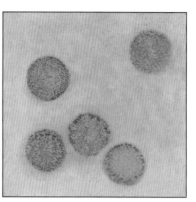
*The Flaviviridae virus*

## Super slaves

Yellow fever scythed through ship after ship sailing from Africa to the New World. Sometimes entire crews perished from yellow fever. On average, one-fifth were done in. When a fever-struck ship arrived in port, it was often quarantined and forced to fly a yellow flag or "jack." Yellow jack became the English maritime name for the disease. As with other mysterious illnesses, Europeans tried fervent prayer and the usual Galenic cures: bleeding, purgatives, enemas, cold-water baths, or aromatic talismans to ward off the miasmas thought to cause the disease. As usual, nothing worked.

Almost as mysterious as yellow fever itself was the fact that enslaved Africans seemed invulnerable to the illness. This was a powerful advantage. When white slavers sickened, blacks could revolt. The famous slave mutiny aboard the ship *Amistad,* for example, was probably made possible by yellow fever. Later, when the disease ravaged Europeans running the plantations of the New World, Africans had multiple opportunities to escape, resist, or attack their tormentors.

How to explain this difference between the races? Whites didn't understand that blacks, having survived yellow fever in Africa as children, now enjoyed lifelong immunity to the disease. Instead, the same people who had once concluded that Native Americans were inferior because they died from European disease now

assured themselves that blacks were suited to slavery because they were immune to yellow fever. The logic of bigotry is a marvelously malleable thing.

## Sweet vengeance

Yellow fever repeatedly harassed European efforts to exploit the Americas. The illness effectively closed the Amazonian basin to European exploitation and repeatedly devastated the plantation economy of the southern United States. (Remarkably, though ships also traveled from Africa to Asia, yellow fever never took hold there.)

One of the earliest New World yellow fever outbreaks was on the British Caribbean island of Barbados. This efficient sugar machine was ravaged by yellow fever from 1647 to 1650 and again in 1690, with over 10,000 people killed.

Even more profitable and more deadly was the French slave colony of Haiti (then called Saint Domingue) on the island of Hispaniola. It is hard to believe that what is now the poorest, most environmentally devastated place in the Western Hemisphere was once the most lucrative colony in the world. Haiti produced more sugar than all the other Caribbean islands combined. It made more money for France than England's revenues from all thirteen American colonies. But in 1789, the French Revolution toppled the monarchy. Ideas of "Liberté! Fraternité! Egalité!" filtered to Haiti. By this time, so many Africans had been imported to the island that slaves now outnumbered their white masters fifteen to one. In 1791, Haiti's slaves revolted. Hundreds of thousands rose up, torched cities, burned plantations, and massacred whites. In 1794, France's revolutionary government abolished slavery throughout the colonies. In 1802, however, France's new ruler, Napoleon Bonaparte, tried to reassert control of Haiti and reestablish slavery. He envisioned an even more profitable colony, supplied with food from France's Louisiana Territory. Napoleon sent a massive amphibious force commanded by his brother-in-law, General Charles leClerc. The soldiers managed to kill over 150,000 slaves. But 50,000 French soldiers also died (including leClerc), mostly from yellow fever.

Imagine trying to fight an enemy impervious to an invisible force that made your comrades become feverish and jaundiced, spew black vomit, and die. The French could sustain neither their morale nor the

*After the African slaves of Haiti revolted and massacred their French masters, Napoleon Bonaparte tried to reassert control. In 1803, his massive amphibious force was defeated. Some 50,000 French soldiers died, mostly from yellow fever.*

invasion. Napoleon went on to acknowledge an independent Haiti, and in 1803 sold France's claim to the now apparently useless Louisiana Territory to the United States.

In 1804, Haiti declared itself a republic. In 1816, the new nation helped the South American general Simón Bolívar mount the invasion that ultimately ended the Spanish empire in the Americas. In return, Bolívar promised to free his own slaves and outlaw slavery in the lands he liberated.

Elsewhere in the Caribbean and the southern United States, slave revolts increased. So did repressive legislation designed to keep slaves in their place, and an abolitionist movement to set them free. One ahead-of-his-time British planter suggested that rethinking the slavery "brand" would solve the problem. Call them "plantation assistants," he suggested, and abolitionists would stop complaining. No one yet realized that with a free Haiti as an example, slavery was finished in the Western Hemisphere. Abolitionist pressure killed British slavery in 1838. The American Civil War drove a stake through the heart of American slavery in 1865. No one thanked yellow fever for starting the revolution.

## Define fiasco

Even after the demise of slavery, yellow fever continued to have an impact on the New World. In 1881, French engineers began construction of a sea-level canal through the Isthmus of Panama. The project was led by renowned French diplomat-impresario Count Ferdinand de Lesseps, who had successfully managed the construction of the Suez Canal across Egypt. Unlike Egypt, however, Panama had a deadly reputation for both malaria and yellow fever. De Lesseps downplayed this problem. To reduce miasmas still thought to cause the disease, the French built tidy, clean, well-built worker barracks with elaborate ornamental gardens. Even before construction began, however, workers started dying from malaria and yellow fever. Since miasma was accounted for, a variety of sin-based explanations were proposed: drinking, gambling, even embezzling were all suspected of causing disease. One engineer, out to prove that immorality was the culprit, brought his upstanding family to Panama. Yellow fever killed them all. Finally, in 1889, with thirty thousand workers dead, billions spent, the canal unbuilt, and de Lesep's reputation in tatters, the project was abandoned.

## A good guess

In 1880, a year before de Lesseps embarked on his Panamanian folly, Dr. Carlos Finlay suggested that *Aedes* mosquitoes might transmit yellow fever. Finlay observed that healthy humans bitten by mosquitoes that had previously fed on yellow fever sufferers also caught the disease. Finlay's hypothesis was ignored for decades, but he was exactly right.

In essence, a mosquito is an airborne syringe. Mosquitoes are equipped with a long hollow proboscis for drinking liquids, a tube for injecting saliva, and a set of cutting stylets for making a wound. Only females use this apparatus to drink blood, and then only when they need to nourish egg production. (For regular meals, mosquitoes drink nectar or honeydew.) When females need a blood meal, they land on a host, poke a hole through the skin, nick a capillary, inject some anticoagulant to make the blood flow, and drink up. Of the 2,500 kinds of mosquitoes, most prefer to dine on other animals. Only a small minority vampirize people. Of the deadly illnesses mosquitoes carry, only a handful affect us. But they're doozies, including malaria, dengue fever, encephalitis, West Nile virus, and yellow fever. Since the Stone Age, the mosquito has probably killed more people than any other creature.

## Walter Reed and Jesse dead

In 1900, during the Spanish-American War, the mystery of yellow fever was finally unraveled. Thousands of American soldiers engaged in the conquest of Cuba had already died from yellow fever when a medical team led by Major Walter Reed arrived to try to determine the cause of the disease. Reed joined three other physicians already at work in Cuba: Jesse Lazear, Aristides Agramonte, and James Carroll. Lazear believed in Carlos Finlay's mosquito-transmission idea. Reed was dubious but allowed Lazear to test the hypothesis. Carroll volunteered to be bitten by a mosquito that had fed on a yellow fever patient. He got sick and recovered. Needing further proof, Lazear allowed himself to be bitten. Two weeks later, he was dead. On October 23, 1900, Walter Reed announced that the *Aedes aegypti* mosquito was

the insect vector (transmitter) for yellow fever.

In Cuba, once the mosquito vector was confirmed, Major General William Crawford Gorgas was charged with its destruction on the island. The female *Aedes* mosquito prefers the moist edges of artificial water containers to lay her eggs. The casks of drinking water taken on board slave ships departing from Africa had transported *Aedes* to the Americas. Now ponds, flower vases, old tires, and other water containers were sustaining the disease. Soldiers under Gorgas's supervision emptied or smashed water containers and sprayed oil on ponds where *Aedes* might breed. Within five months, these methods had eliminated yellow fever from Cuba. Gorgas was a hero. In 1904, he was dispatched to the American revival of the Panama Canal project. By 1906, using the same methods, Gorgas had eradicated yellow fever there, too.

It would not be until 1927 that the South African physician Max Theiler and his colleagues would prove that yellow fever was caused by a Flaviviridae virus and eventually develop a successful vaccine. Called 17D, it is still used today. Later, scientists learned where yellow fever hid in between epidemics: the African virus has found a permanent reservoir in the New World tropics among populations of tree-dwelling monkeys and their mosquito parasites. High above humans in the forest canopy, the virus cycles between insect and animal. As long as the forest is undisturbed, yellow fever remains "silent" for years or even decades. But each time a tree is cut to clear more land for habitation or agriculture, yellow fever may crash back to earth, ready to reenter the human population chain.

But what about yellow fever's impact in the white man's grave? Africans suffered from the disease but were not insensitive to its deadly effects on their colonial masters. While whites saw yellow fever as an obstacle to control, Africans recognized it as an ally in their struggles for freedom and independence. Well into the 1980s, these words were still chanted by many African schoolchildren: ". . . Only mosquito can save Africa. Only malaria can save Africa. Only yellow fever can save Africa."

The African Flaviviridae virus has found a permanent reservoir in tree-dwelling New World primates, like these howler monkeys, and their mosquito parasites. When the tropical rain forest is cut down, the pathogens of the canopy may come into contact with people, giving yellow fever a chance to reenter the human infection chain.

# Harsh Teacher
*How cholera cleaned up cities*

The Blue Fever
The spread of cholera
1817-1863

First pandemic
Second pandemic
Third pandemic

## Repeat after me

You know the drill: wipe, wash, don't forget to flush. We learn the habits of personal hygiene from our parents, in school, on the job, and from the media. They seem basic, natural, obvious—even scientific. But they didn't start that way. A little over a century ago, cleanliness and sanitation were still radical notions resisted by just about everyone. It took several global pandemics to change people's habits.

In 1817, a new disease swept out of India. It caused a violent, gushing diarrhea and vomiting that within a few hours could turn a healthy human being into a shriveled, blue-tinged corpse. No one knew what caused the illness. No one understood how it was spread. What people *did* know was that it didn't discriminate: rich or poor, anyone who contracted the disease was likely to die. In seven separate pandemics over 180 years, it traveled to every continent except Antarctica, killing millions of people. Along the way it was given many names: hyperanthraxis, spasmodic cholera, Asiatic cholera, convulsive nervous cholera, cholera asphyxia, malignant cholera, the blue cholera, the blue fever, the blue vomit, the yellow wind, the plague, the pestilence, the black illness.

Today we call it simply cholera. Simply put, it has been one of the most influential diseases of modern times. Cholera highlighted the desperate poverty and ghastly living conditions of newly industrialized Europe and America. It laid bare the threads connecting poverty to wealth. It settled the argument between two contending theories of disease, miasma and contagion. Most importantly, it catalyzed the development of modern sanitation, which enabled huge numbers of people to live together in close quarters and remain healthy, making the modern city possible. Sanitation is also partially responsible for the human population explosion. About one billion people inhabited our planet in 1800. We're over six billion and counting today.

## Feeling blue

For most of the nineteenth century, people didn't know what caused cholera. *Miasmists*—followers of the ancient theories of Galen—blamed the disease on mysterious emanations: electrical currents ("the miasmic electric effluvium"), rotting garbage, foul-smelling sewers, and puzzling swamp vapors. *Contagionists* believed cholera was spread by contact with an infectious agent: bad cucumbers, bad beer, foreign food, shellfish, phosphorus, copper, sulfur, or other contaminants.

Cures and preventatives were varied and contradictory. Several towns tried quarantines. Others experimented with noise: cannons were blasted, muskets fired, gongs banged, and shouts raised from sunrise to sunset. Several nations tried closing their borders to all travelers. Many individuals tried waist-hugging flannel cholera belts. Entrepreneurs made fortunes selling cholera brandy and cholera drops. Doctors prescribed hot poultices of salt, mustard,

Nineteenth-century industrial cities were fetid sties, mounded with garbage and human waste. Rivers served as both sewers and sources of drinking water, spreading cholera and other diseases. People died at rates rivaling those associated with the Black Death.

roasted black pepper, powdered ginger, scraped horse-radish, or burnt cork. They also recommended ice-water baths, boiling-water baths, tobacco enemas, opium suppositories, and the ever-popular phlebotomy. England twice tried a National Day of Prayer and Deliverance. Nothing worked.

## The price of empire

We can blame the British for the spread of cholera. Like other empires before them, the British invaded and connected areas that had previously been isolated from one another. Cholera is endemic to India, killing unnumbered thousands in repeated epidemics since at least 400 B.C. It even has its own goddess on the sub-continent, Hulka Devi. The first cholera pandemic began in 1817, when Britain was in the process of con-quering the subcontinent. British soldiers stationed near Calcutta contracted cholera and carried the disease across the Himalayas to the Nepalese and Afghans they were fighting along India's northern bor-der. From there, cholera was relayed overland to Burma and Thailand and by sea to Sumatra, Java, China, Japan, Malaya, the Philippines, and Arabia. Slave traders carried the disease south from Oman to Zanzibar. It also migrated up the Persian Gulf to south-ern Russia. In each of these regions, thousands, some-times tens of thousands, died in a matter of days. The winter of 1823–24 halted the advance.

The second cholera pandemic started in Bengal in 1826. By 1830, cholera had reached Moscow. By September 1831, the disease was in Islam's holiest city, Mecca. (It became one of the established dangers of the Muslim pilgrimage, reappearing forty times between 1831 and 1912.) That same year, it reached Berlin and Hamburg.

A strict quarantine might have stopped cholera there. But in England, nothing was supposed to stand in the way of the free exchange of goods and services. Businessmen thwarted an attempted quarantine to keep out ships that had visited infected German ports. Soon cholera started sickening people in the English town of Sunderland. Again, business inter-ests argued against quarantine: it would hurt profits, it would cause unemployment. Sunderland was re-opened. Cholera spread through England and Ireland, then jumped the Atlantic to North America. Again, tens of thousands died.

## Drink up

We now know something that nineteenth-century people did not: cholera is spread by contaminated water. A look at living conditions in that era helps explain cholera's global reach. In England, for exam-ple, the population was at an all-time high. People were pouring in from the countryside to towns and cities in search of higher wages. Thousands of workers were jammed into cramped, dark, poorly ventilated housing. Why dark? Since 1696, the Window Tax imposed a duty on dwellings with more than six win-dows. Clear glass was a luxury. To show off their

*Cholera became one of the established dangers of the Muslim pilgrimage, reappearing forty times between 1831 and 1912, until strict sanitation, vaccination, and quarantine were practiced. Here, cholera victims are unloaded at the port of Jaffa.*

wealth, the super-rich demanded homes with as many windows as structurally possible. Landlords, on the other hand, and even some members of the middle class, installed few windows. They even bricked over windows in some buildings to stay below the taxable number. People rarely washed their hands in those days, and in their gloomy, stuffy homes, they couldn't see well enough to clean.

Sanitation was inadequate to nonexistent. Although flush toilets had been used in England since at least the sixteenth century (Queen Elizabeth I got hers in 1597), most human waste was disposed of in pit outhouses. A landlord might provide one over-burdened, rarely emptied privy to serve thirty families. When it overflowed, fecal matter was deposited elsewhere: in cellars, in ditches, or in the street. In London, human waste would eventually end up draining into the Thames River, a malodorous sewer nicknamed "the Big Stink" that was also the final repository of butchers' offal, tannery effluent, and household garbage. It was the city's main source of drinking water.

Under such conditions, disease was rampant. Aside from cholera, people suffered from "summer diarrhea" and epidemics of waterborne typhoid, lice-borne typhus, tuberculosis, influenza, and more. People died at rates not seen since the Black Death. Cities needed a continuous flow of new people from the relatively healthy countryside just to keep their population level. No wonder large families were encouraged.

Death rates were highest among the poor. They ate bad food and got little of it. They lived in small, poorly constructed, hard-to-heat dwellings awash in human waste. They wore the threadbare castoffs of their betters. Ill-fed, ill-housed, and ill-clothed, their immune systems compromised, it is no wonder the poor died young. Britain's upper classes assured themselves that this grotesque disparity was divinely ordained. Poverty was not an economic or social problem but a spiritual condition, a punishment for sin. With the passage of the 1832 Anatomy Act, poverty also became, in effect, a crime. Postmortem dissection by surgeons, anatomists, and medical students, formerly a punishment inflicted only on the very worst condemned criminals, now became instead the fate of paupers unable to pay for their own burials. The Poor Law Amendment of 1834 tightened the noose, outlawing cash charity to the unemployed poor and forcing them into the prison-like workhouse—even orphans, the elderly, and the disabled.

Edwin Chadwick, a reforming civil servant, documented the conditions affecting the poor with his *Report on the Sanitary Condition of the Labouring Population of Great Britain,* presented to Parliament in 1842. Chadwick asserted that the squalid existence of Britain's poor was involuntary. He compared it unfavorably to American slavery. Chadwick also revealed that country people lived longer than townsfolk. In a city like Leeds, laborers could expect to die, on average, at age seventeen. Tradesmen died in their mid-twenties. Even the privileged gentry usually survived only into their forties. You might make more money in a city, but you wouldn't live long to enjoy it.

## Next they'll want health insurance

Chadwick, who lived to be ninety, thought this a waste. He was an advocate of utilitarianism, the belief that government should act to create "the greatest happiness of the greatest number." He argued that better living conditions would allow poor people to work harder and be less of a burden on society. Chadwick was also a miasmist. He declared that "all smell is disease." Get rid of the smell, Chadwick reasoned, and you get rid of the disease. He recommended improved housing, paved streets, clean drinking water, flush toilets, and efficient sewers for everyone. Opponents called this "mawkish philanthropy," but after years of bickering and thousands more cholera deaths, Parliament began to implement Chadwick's reforms with the first Public Health Act of 1848. The Window Tax was repealed in 1851. The third cholera pandemic started in 1853, killing fifteen thousand people in England alone. It helped spur the Sanitary Act of 1866, the second Public Health Act of 1872, and the third Public Health Act of 1875.

## Check out the apron on that guy

Just as important as Chadwick in the prevention of cholera was Ignaz Semmelweis's advocacy of hand washing. In 1846, Semmelweis was a Hungarian obstetrician working in Vienna. It is hard to believe now, but in those days even well-off Europeans rarely washed their hands. No wonder: not all homes or businesses had piped-in water, and hot water had to be heated on a stove. With knowledge of microbial pathogens still in the future, the need for regular, systematic hand washing wasn't understood. Semmelweis, however, pointed out that women who gave birth with midwives (or even on the street) had a

*Ignaz Semmelweis introduced modern hand washing into his maternity wards. He dropped the death rate from thirty out of a hundred to one.*

much better chance of survival than those who delivered their babies in crowded hospitals, where doctors worked ungloved and wore the same attire throughout the day. For surgeons, bloody aprons were a sign of professional prowess—the redder the better. Semmelweis suggested that physicians were passing a fatal "something" from sick and newly dead patients to healthy mothers. Although doctors were incensed at the accusation that they were contagious, Semmelweis ordered his subordinates to wash their hands in chlorinated water before entering his wards. The maternal death rate dropped from 30 percent to 1 percent. The Semmelweis technique spread from hospitals to businesses,

schools, and homes as a cheap, effective way to stop illness. It still is.

Though the Chadwick reforms and the Semmelweis method improved urban life expectancy and helped curb cholera, the disease remained a huge health problem. In 1854, a London physician named John Snow noticed that in Soho many cholera deaths were concentrated around the Broad Street public pump. To see if water pollution was the cause, he removed the handle so that the pump could not be used. Neighborhood cholera deaths plummeted. Eventually Snow compiled a detailed survey of the many competing companies that supplied water to London, each with its own overlapping systems of pipes. He conclusively connected cholera with the sewage-contaminated drinking water of one company, drawn downriver from London. More investigation showed that of London's eight private water companies, only five filtered their water. (One customer found his pipes clogged by a rotting eel!) Snow was attacked for his ideas by miasma-obsessed sanitationists, who feared his focus on waterborne contagion would slow the cleanup of the English slums. But by 1902, London had merged its private water companies into a single municipal corporation that supplied everyone in the city with filtered, chlorine-treated water. Cholera and other waterborne diseases faded. Health improved.

These changes were noted and copied elsewhere. In Germany, renowned pathologist Rudolph Virchow designed a new sewer system for Berlin. In the United States, Dr. John H. Griscom adapted Chadwick's theme and title for his influential 1845 tract, *The Sanitary Condition of the Laboring Population of New York*. Jacob Riis's 1890 blockbuster, *How the Other Half Lives*, also helped ignite American reform. Across Europe and America, and later Japan and other parts of the industrializing world, cities were transformed from fetid sties to livable metropolises with improved housing, efficient sewers, clean piped water, and regular garbage removal.

To understand the importance of these changes, one has only to look at the fate of an industrial nation denied the basics of modern life. Iraq is an instructive example. Though the dictator Saddam Hussein ruled Iraq for much of the late twentieth century, the country was modern and prosperous, with a large, educated middle class concentrated in cities like Baghdad, Fallujah, and Basra. In the 1990s, however, the United Nations implemented sanctions that denied Iraq critical water treatment system parts and medical supplies the Iraqi government might have also been able to use to manufacture weapons. The health effects were immediate, widespread, and ghastly. Infant mortality rose sharply. Infectious diseases spread. Cholera returned. In all, about a million Iraqi children died. Any other industrial country denied essential modern sanitation would suffer a similar outcome.

## Have vibrio, will travel

Thirty years, two cholera pandemics, and hundreds of thousands of deaths after John Snow's observations, the great German biologist Robert Koch finally discovered the microbe responsible for cholera. In 1883, during the fifth pandemic (1881–86), Koch beat his archrival, Louis Pasteur, by identifying the cholera vibrio in the disease's homeland, India. Koch became a German national hero. (*Vibrio* is one of the many shape-based words still used to describe bacteria. A vibrio is comma-shaped. A bacillus is rod-shaped. A spirochete is screw-shaped. A coccus is round.)

In Koch's day, cholera's life cycle was a mystery. Today we know that vibrios adhere to the lining of the small intestine, where they multiply and excrete a

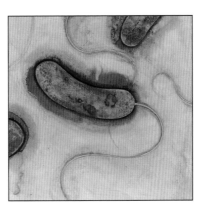

*The bacterium* Vibrio cholerae

toxin that prevents intestinal cells from efficiently absorbing water and causes the body to lose water and salt into the intestines. Cholera diarrhea can range from mild to deadly. In extreme cases the host is so dehydrated that blood thickens to a tarlike consistency and the skin is tinted the telltale blue. Blood pressure plummets, and the host dies.

We now understand that cholera vibrios can survive for years in a sporelike state on the bodies of copepods, millimeter-sized crustaceans that feed on algae. At one time this trio of organisms—vibrios, copepods, and algae—coexisted mostly in the Bay of Bengal. When water temperatures rose and enough nutrients were available, algae would bloom, and copepod and vibrio populations grew. If a tropical cyclone, tsunami, or other event caused this cholera-rich seawater to contaminate inland drinking-water supplies, cholera could reenter the human infection chain. But today ships have sucked up Bay of Bengal ballast water and spewed it out around the world, introducing the bacteria to other areas. Three different strains of the cholera vibrio now compete for dominance. The Classic strain is deadly but susceptible to disinfectants such as chlorine. It is now rarely encountered. The newer El Tor

strain causes a milder illness but is more resistant to chlorine. It is now the most common strain by far. The hybrid Bengal strain is both deadly and resistant.

## So cheap yet so far

Cholera remains a formidable illness. It would girdle the earth in a sixth pandemic that lasted from 1899 to 1909. A seventh—not yet over—began in 1961 in Indonesia. Unlike the cholera of Chadwick's day, however, the disease is now a preventable, curable illness. We can treat and filter water to make it safe to drink. We can rehydrate cholera victims with water mixed with special salts and sugars. Nearly everyone so treated survives. Cholera should be history. Indeed, if all governments applied Chadwick's recommendation of universal sanitation, cholera *would* be history. That cholera remains a health problem at all is testament to our continuing unwillingness to seriously grapple with its root cause: global poverty.

Today a billion people around the world still lack access to improved water supplies such as piped systems, capped wells, and springs. Hundreds of millions more rely on water sources that, though improved, are still contaminated and unsafe. Two billion have no way of properly disposing of human waste. Two million to three million children die annually of waterborne diseases, including cholera. This problem could be fixed for $10 billion to $20 billion a year for fifteen years. That's less than a third of the $61 billion Americans spend annually on soft drinks. We're not talking fancy indoor plumbing, just basic water treatment and latrines for everyone on earth.

One temporary solution to this hygiene nightmare is the U.S. Centers for Disease Control's Safe Water System (SWS). This cheap, hardy, easy-to-use water-purification system has been deployed in twenty-two countries on three continents. It has been used in refugee camps, disaster areas, war zones, rural villages, and urban slums. It relies on a simple idea: bottle inexpensive chlorine for people to use to treat water stored in the home and keep the water in a closed, narrow-neck plastic bottle that, unlike traditional wide-mouthed containers, cannot easily be recontaminated by unclean hands. This is no permanent cure for contaminated water. It's a stopgap. Until the next Edwin Chadwick comes along, however, a stopgap will have to do.

# Dying Hope
## How tuberculosis changed from chic to shameful

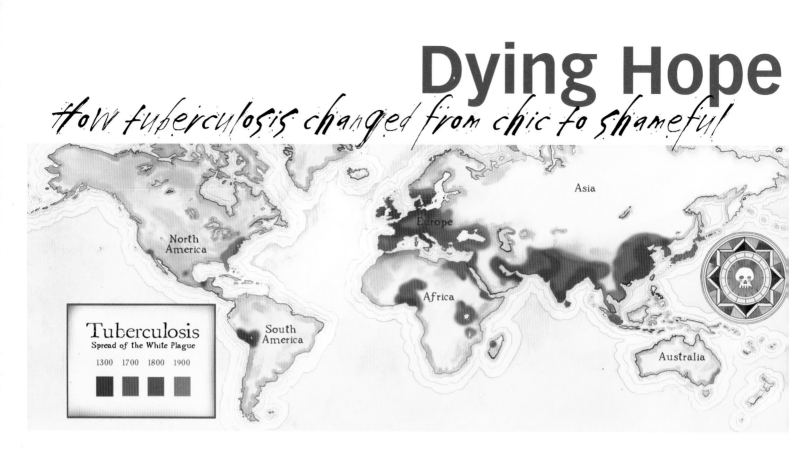

Tuberculosis
**Spread of the White Plague**

1300   1700   1800   1900

## Prove it

As we have seen in previous chapters, disease is a screen on which we project our deepest fears, hopes, and prejudices. So it was with tuberculosis, an ancient illness that became epidemic during the nineteenth century at the same time a new cultural movement—Romanticism—was catching fire. In the growing cities of the industrial world, Romantic beliefs and tubercular symptoms intersected and reinforced one another. For a time, tuberculosis was welcomed in some households, envied in others, as a sure sign of creative genius. Eventually Romantic tuberculosis would completely upend ruling-class beliefs about beauty and status. But once TB's real cause was understood, the disease's reputation soured. TB became associated with poverty, overcrowding, and bad hygiene. Thus stigmatized, it became a powerful catalyst for the creation of modern public health systems, a control on both the disease and the poor people seen to be its carriers.

## That graveyard cough

Tuberculosis is caused by a bacterium. It appeared in human populations about fifteen thousand years ago, probably jumping to us from cattle when people began to domesticate livestock. TB did its work not in days or weeks but over years, striking when age, poor nutrition, overwork, or illness compromised a person's immune system. TB robbed the body of energy, progressed to spasmodic coughing, advanced to hacking up blood and bits of lung, and ended in a gasping, lingering death. There was no cure. One could survive to old age, but most TB victims died young. TB thrived in crowded conditions, where the microbe could easily pass from person to person. It flourished in slums and sweatshops where people were ill fed and overworked and ventilation was poor. By the early 1800s, TB was killing about a quarter of all Europeans. Later, when Asia industrialized, TB death rates there were just as bad.

The ancient Greeks called TB *phthisis*, a term that compares the inexorable destruction of the body's vitality to the waning of the moon. The seventeenth-century English religious writer John Bunyan called tuberculosis "the Captain of all these Men of Death." In the nineteenth century, the most common term for TB was consumption. It was also called pleural abscess, hectic fever, the white plague, the graveyard cough, inflammation of the lung, delicacy of the lungs, lung weakness, and complaint of the chest. Crucially, in much of the industrial West, consumption was thought to be hereditary, not contagious. Thus, most TB sufferers were not quarantined. They mixed freely with the uninfected, ensuring the spread of the disease.

Although tuberculosis of the lungs was the most common form of the illness, the bacterium could also manifest itself in other parts of the body with different symptoms and different names. Tuberculosis of the neck was called the king's evil and scrofula. Tuberculosis of the bones was called the white swelling. Tuberculosis of

The Romantics believed tuberculosis signified artistic fire. Pale skin, flushed cheeks, and the bloody handkerchief were envied marks of passion and genius.

the stomach was called mesenteric disease. Tuberculosis of the spine was called Pott's disease. Tuberculosis of the skin was called *lupus vulgaris*. The term "tuberculosis" itself was coined in the early nineteenth century. It refers to the tiny inflamed scars on the lungs, called tubercles, that are a sure sign of the disease.

## The Age of Reason

To understand how nineteenth-century tuberculosis became a popular disease, the beliefs of the day need to be understood. At the beginning of the nineteenth century, Enlightenment values exerted a profound effect on the intellectual life of Europe and America. The universe, formerly chaotic and terrible, was now seen as orderly, comprehensible, and measurable. Reason trumped religious faith. Atheism was trendy. Scientific progress ruled. In the arts, Classicism stressed order, calm, harmony, balance, and of course rationality.

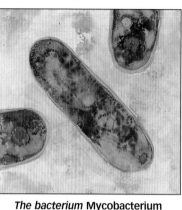
*The bacterium* Mycobacterium tuberculosis

But this new thinking papered over ancient ideas about health and illness. The sick were still bled to rebalance bodily humors. Most people still thought appearance and disease were outward signs of inner character. A beautiful person was good. An ugly person was bad. A light-skinned person was superior to a dark one. One way new thinking and old mixed was a popular pseudoscience called phrenology. Practitioners claimed that personality, character, and intelligence could be determined by the systematic study of the shape and size of a person's head. This was simply social prejudice and racism tricked out to look and sound like rational thought. In truth, it was nonsense.

Appearance and disease were perceived not just as outer markers of inner truth but as signifiers of class. In an age when food was scarce and famine was always a possibility, body fat was a good thing, a sign of wealth. One of the diseases brought on by the beef-and-burgundy diet of the wealthy was gout, a painful inflammation of the joints. It was a mark of distinction, like a Lexus or a Rolex today. The writer Edward Gibbon, a poor man made fat and rich by his acclaimed six-volume *History of the Decline and Fall of the Roman Empire,* was proud of his gout. He bragged about it to his friends.

## Consuming passion

Romantics rebelled against Enlightenment ideals. They worshiped self-expression and imagination.

They loathed the ideals of Classicism. They sought freedom from social conventions. But Romantics were also people of their time, and they believed that illness and appearance revealed inner truth. They adored TB.

Romantics were intoxicated with sensation and thought the well-lived life was bright, intense, and snuffed out in the bloom of youth. For them, TB was a badge of passion and genius. In a tubercular family of artists or writers, consumption in the children might be taken as a sign that they had inherited their parents' creative talents. The best-known symptoms of the disease were inflamed cheeks, pallid skin (popular since ancient Roman times as a sign of genius), the coughing up of blood, and a thin, "consumed" body. These signs were thought to be manifestations of an inner artistic fire. Some people believed TB ignited the flames. Even doctors were influenced by Romanticism. One of the terms they used for TB was *spes moribunda,* Latin for "dying hope." This referred to the flushed cheeks of the terminal consumptive, giving the false impression of good health.

Death was a prevalent theme in Romantic writing. The Graveyard School of poetry celebrated death, nights, ruins, churchyards, and ghosts. One of the most popular themes was a veiled widow in black mourning dress. The poet John Keats died at age twenty-five from TB. One of his most famous poems is "Ode to a Nightingale," which describes the agony of a dying patient.

In painting, the Pre-Raphaelite Brotherhood obsessed over morbidity, usually showing models who were wistful, lonely, dispirited, and tubercular. Flaming redheads were especially popular subjects. Indeed, Elizabeth Siddall and Jane Burden, two of the favorite pre-Raphaelite models, actually had TB.

Other Romantic tuberculars include the writers Robert Louis Stevenson, Jane Austen, and the three Brontë sisters; the philosopher Henry David Thoreau; the artist Aubrey Beardsley; and the composer Frédéric Chopin. Some lived for a long time, but all did their work in the knowledge that their lives might be cut short by consumption. Not all artistic types got TB, of course, however much they might wish for the disease. The poet Lord Byron was a fanatical dieter whose obsession with extra flesh bordered on anorexia. He thought consumption would make him more attractive to women. "Look at that poor Byron," he imagined them saying. "How interesting he looks in dying."

Eventually this cult of youth and consumptive thinness began to resonate beyond Romantic circles, even reshaping ideals of the pudgy upper class. By the twentieth century, food was becoming plentiful and cheap in the industrial world, so a big waistline no longer had snob appeal. Instead, the long necks, bright eyes, rosy cheeks, and emaciated bodies of tubercular Romanticism became the elite standard, especially among upper-class women like American socialite, Nazi sympathizer, and wannabe queen of England Wallis Simpson. She announced that "one can never be too rich or too thin." Today the tubercular look remains popular in the fashion industry's unflagging obsession with malnourished models. Even young girls feel the pressure to emulate consumptive scrawniness. Early on they learn the premium society places on appearance—and may feel that to be popular and considered pretty, they need to be skinny. Ironically, in the supersized industrial world, it is not the rich but the fast-food-fed poor who are the fattest class of all.

Western ideas about Romantic tuberculosis have parallels in Asia. In the eighteenth-century Chinese novel *The Dream of the Red Chamber*, the heroine, Lin Tai-yu, dies of TB at the moment her sweetheart marries another woman. In Japan, writers and some doctors called TB "lovesickness." It was thought to be an illness brought on by longing or frustration that made people more intelligent and passionate. Love-starved daughters and diligent boys studying the Chinese classics were considered most susceptible. Tokutomi Roka's

*In Japan, tuberculosis was thought to be lovesickness.*

1898 novel *Hototogisu* ("Nightingale") is about a young wife miraculously cured of her terminal tuberculosis when her beloved husband returns from abroad. This hugely popular book has been the subject of several films, many dramas, and a hit song. It is but one example of a Japanese literary genre that revolves around tuberculosis.

## The romance is gone

Tuberculosis lost its romantic status once the true cause of the disease was understood. After the publication of Pasteur's *Germ Theory of Disease* in 1880, researchers raced to discover one infectious microbe after another. In March 1882, after eight months of effort, Robert Koch finally isolated the TB bacterium. Consumption, it turned out, wasn't hereditary at all. The Koch bacillus was a rod-shaped microbe that passed from person to person suspended in microscopic droplets of saliva from a person's sneeze or cough. It could be avoided but not cured.

Confronted with this new knowledge, the middle class became obsessed with cleanliness, sure that TB microbes were lurking everywhere. Bodily fluids became scary, human smells repulsive (the search for effective underarm deodorants and antiperspirants starts here). Spitting, kissing, and even talking were now seen as bacteriological menaces. One story told of the tubercular worker who licked his fingers while he turned the pages of documents, spreading consumption far and wide. One British sign from that era reads, "Don't Spit! It's Disgusting and It Spreads Germs!"

In the United States, control of tuberculosis was first systematized in New York City. By 1900, Dr. Herman Biggs of the Metropolitan Board of Health had developed the basic procedures still used for the control of TB around the world. These included free sputum exams, mandatory reporting of cases, mandatory isolation and treatment of those infected, education of the public about the disease, and monitoring of living conditions. The methods were despotic by today's standards, and the system concentrated on the poor, by now stigmatized and stereotyped as society's primary TB carriers. Biggs proceeded from the notion that still animates all public health systems: the well-being of society is more important than private liberty. Since he was focusing on people with little political or economic clout, few objected. By contrast, the middle class and wealthy enjoyed private medicine, where the well-being of the individual comes first. The two systems, public and private, developed separately, in tandem.

Restrictions on the individual reached their apex with the creation of the sanitarium, an institution that totally cut off consumptives from society, sometimes voluntarily, sometimes mandatorily, sometimes for years, sometimes for life. If one was rich, a sanitarium might be a fancy seaside spa or a mountain resort. If one was poor, a sanitarium was little better than a prison. By 1950, over a hundred thousand sanitarium beds existed in the United States alone. Sanitarium doctors experimented with an amazing variety of therapies to try to treat TB. These included bed rest, fresh air, lung collapse, rib removal, exposure to heat, exposure to cold, exposure to sun, gold therapy, calcium therapy, iodine therapy, horse riding, the milk cure, the grape cure, the wine cure, and cod-liver oil. Dietary

therapies ranged from strict limits on what a patient could eat to stuffing them with nutritious food. For society, the main benefit was the removal of infectious individuals.

Meanwhile, a new social reform movement, moral environmentalism, lobbied for better housing for the poor, public parks, public schools, hospitals, efficient waste disposal, sewers, water systems, street cleaning, and the regulation of markets, slaughterhouses, and restaurants. The idea was simple and owes much to Edwin Chadwick: improve the environment and you improve the person. The combination of control, isolation, diet, and improved living conditions worked. In 1828, TB deaths in England were about four thousand per million. By 1948, TB deaths in the United States had dropped to about four hundred per million. With the advent of antibiotics—drugs that could actually kill the tuberculosis bacterium—the American TB death rate dropped to its lowest ever: ninety per million. The tuberculosis decline among American minorities was not so steep. Indeed, in many developing nations, rates had not declined at all. Nevertheless, the mood was so optimistic that in 1980, a panel of experts convened by the U.S. Congress was called the Advisory Committee for the Elimination of Tuberculosis. In retrospect, this seems astoundingly naive.

*Before an antibiotic cure for tuberculosis was discovered, daily doses of fresh air were considered vital to preventing and treating the disease, even in the coldest weather.*

## Back with a vengeance

Once TB was no longer a terror, tuberculosis control systems deteriorated. In the United States during the 1980s, sanitariums were shut down or converted into hospitals. Public health programs were defunded. Salaries stagnated for personnel responsible for monitoring and treating TB. Funding for poverty programs was slashed. Mental hospitals were emptied, pushing people unable to care for themselves onto the street or into crowded homeless shelters. In 1992, the Soviet Union collapsed and with it the expensive TB control program of SanEp, the Russian empire's unwieldy state health system. Revolution in Africa and Central America ensured that people there with tuberculosis got partial treatment or no treatment.

Under such conditions, many TB patients took only enough antibiotics to feel better but not enough to eradicate all the TB germs in their bodies. They killed off the weak bacteria, allowing the strong ones to reproduce and make them sick again. The next time they took the antibiotic, it didn't work. The strong microbes were *resistant*. These resistant TB bacteria spread around the world in the bodies of refugees fleeing their crumbling societies. In 1993, the reemergence of tuberculosis caused the World Health Organization to proclaim a global TB emergency. Today nearly two billion people on earth may host the tuberculosis bacterium. Over the next decade, ninety million will develop active TB. Eventually thirty million will die.

Tuberculosis, once the most Romantic of illnesses, is now the deadliest disease on earth. Controlling the bacterium is the twenty-first century's greatest public health challenge.

# Purple Death Watch
## How influenza influenced War

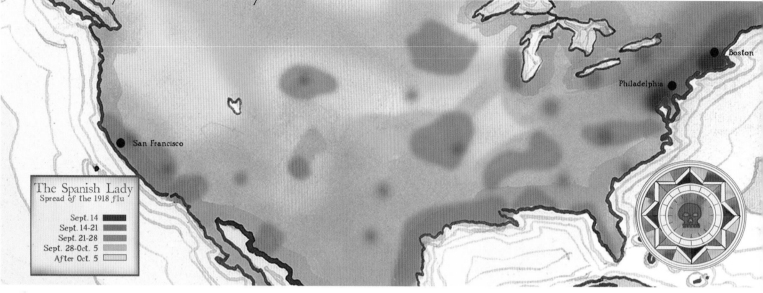

The Spanish Lady
Spread of the 1918 flu

Sept. 14
Sept. 14-21
Sept. 21-28
Sept. 28-Oct. 5
After Oct. 5

Boston

Philadelphia

San Francisco

## The sausage machine

World War I extinguished ideals of chivalry that since medieval times had cloaked battle in a nimbus of glory, honor, and sacrifice. In this, the world's first truly industrial war, battle was revealed not as a righteous conflict but as a riot of slaughter. Most of the efficient mass killing machines we are familiar with today got their start here: tanks, long-range artillery, machine guns, aerial bombardment, submarines, and poison gas. In the horrific trench warfare that characterized this struggle, tens of thousands of soldiers lost their lives to win a few feet of ground. Tens of thousands more died to win it back. The war had many names, including "the Great War" and "the war to end all wars." President Woodrow Wilson's favorite was "the war to make the world safe for democracy." Poet Robert Graves called it "the sausage machine," because "it was fed with live men, churned out corpses, and remained firmly screwed in place." From 1914 to 1918, over fifteen million people died, nine million of them in combat.

In the last months of the war, however, a new killer appeared, far more efficient than anything devised by man. It was Spanish influenza, the single largest epidemic of the twentieth century, if not world history. As with normal flu, people who caught this illness became lethargic, feverish, and achy. But instead of recovering, many of those who were infected by this strain of influenza then progressed to a deadly pneumonia that filled the lungs with bloody froth. Oxygen

was sucked from the tissues, turning the skin a sickly purple before the victim died, gasping for air.

Spanish flu had another fatal peculiarity. Most flu epidemics kill the very young or the very old. This disease, however, was most lethal among those it was most likely to encounter on the battlefields of Europe: twenty-to-thirty-year-olds. Of the one hundred thousand American soldiers who died in World War I, forty-three thousand died from the Spanish flu. Total U.S. flu deaths were about half a million. Globally, death toll estimates range from twenty million to one hundred million people. Up to twenty million may have died in India alone. In some of the isolated aboriginal populations in Alaska and the Pacific, nearly everyone perished.

"The Purple Death" didn't just kill huge numbers of people; it shaped world events. The epidemic was a major player in the final battles of World War I and had a role in the shaping of the Versailles peace treaty. It totally overwhelmed the ability of even the best-prepared governments to care for the living and bury the dead. It catalyzed the creation of today's global influenza surveillance system and the cycle of annual autumn flu shots. Most important of all, scientific research into the nature of the Spanish flu uncovered something totally new and unexpected that would revolutionize medicine: the first antibiotic.

## A bloody chessboard

Politically, economically, and socially, World War I was an epochal event that demolished the existing

*In San Francisco, during the height of the epidemic, masked revelers celebrated the armistice that ended World War I.*

order and created many of the conflicts we live with today. When the war started in August 1914, Europe was a patchwork of ancient, tottering monarchies and empires, stitched together by intermarriage and allied against one another by secret treaties. It ended in November 1918 with armistice: the theatrical "eleventh hour of the eleventh day of the eleventh month." Czarist Russia had collapsed, the Soviet Union was born, and the Ottoman and Austro-Hungarian empires were dismantled. Iraq was created out of several Ottoman provinces. Palestine was made a British mandate, paving the way for the creation of the State of Israel and its attendant problems. Imperial Germany, on whom the entire disaster was blamed, was humiliated, stripped of its colonies, and saddled with crushing reparations.

## The blame on Spain

World War I was a disease-conscious war. Only nine years before, the Russo-Japanese War (the first major conflict that occurred after the discoveries of Pasteur and Koch) had shown that with proper sanitation among the troops, deaths from disease could be less than those from combat. This was significant: in nearly all past military conflicts, more soldiers died from infectious disease than from battle. With this example in mind, military leaders on both sides in the Great War took extraordinary precautions to prevent epidemics among their troops. They were especially concerned about typhus, a bacterial disease carried by fleas and human body lice. It thrives in conditions where people cannot bathe regularly or change their clothes. At the beginning of the war, both armies were especially vigilant about delousing soldiers returning from the front lines. In Serbia, however, sanitation broke down. During 1914 alone, a typhus epidemic there killed over two hundred thousand people. After the war, that disease spread to the freshly minted Soviet Union, where in four years it killed ten million people. Lenin is said to have remarked, "Either socialism will defeat the louse or the louse will defeat socialism." (Socialism won.) As bad as typhus was, however, the flu was worse. No army had ever encountered a disease as murderous as the "Spanish Lady."

The flu was called Spanish not because it started in Spain but because it was first reported in newspapers there. Why? Because Spain remained neutral in the

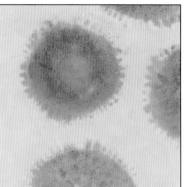

*The influenza virus*

war and therefore its military didn't censor the press. People were getting sick everywhere, but in the nations at war—including the United States—any news that might help the enemy was suppressed.

The first *recorded* incidence of Spanish flu was in the United States at Fort Riley, Kansas, in March 1918. This first spring wave of the flu epidemic was a mild three-day illness that caused aches, fever, chills, a red face, and a weeklong hangover. As it spread to the war zone, doctors called this spring flu a "delightful disease" (everybody ill, nobody dying), but the soldiers weren't nearly so grateful. The French griped about *la grippe*. The British suffered from "three-day fever." The Italians complained of "sand fly fever." The Americans came down with "knock-me-down fever."

Mild it might have been, but the first wave arrived at a critical time for Germany. When General Erich Ludendorff first heard that the enemy was suffering from what the Germans called *Blitzkatarrh* ("lightning flu"), he informed Kaiser Wilhelm II that it might help the war effort. But when German soldiers started coming down with the very same complaint, General Ludendorff blamed the failure of his July *Friedensturm*, or "peace offensive," on the disease. This decisive battle had been Germany's last real chance at victory. Afterward, American soldiers poured into Europe, ensuring victory for the Allies. Though the conflict would rage on for many more months in 1918, the outcome was essentially decided.

## Gauze, laws, and paws

By July 1918, the first mild wave of the epidemic had faded around the world. In August, the second lethal wave of the disease appeared simultaneously among troops in Sierra Leone, France, and Massachusetts. It quickly spread. In the United States, though thousands started dying every week from the flu, Americans were more interested in war than illness. They took many actions that unwittingly spread the disease. Thousands of soldiers were shuttled around the country from base to base. Tens of thousands of men lined up to register for the draft. Hundreds of thousands packed together for Liberty Loan Bond parades to raise money for the war. By September, nearly every major American city was infected. In most cities the epidemic lasted for a month or so.

At the Philadelphia morgue during the flu epidemic, bodies were stacked four deep in the halls.

Some cities had two or three waves of illness.

San Francisco had ample warning to prepare for the worst. The height of the West Coast epidemic lagged about a month behind that on the eastern seaboard. Officials were able to read newspaper accounts from unprepared cities like Philadelphia. Understaffed hospitals there had been flooded with patients. The city morgue (capacity thirty-six) had overflowed, with hundreds of decomposing bodies stacked four deep in the halls. The bereaved were made to dig the graves of their dead, and funeral homes doubled their fees. In preparation for the inevitable, San Francisco ordered extra coffins and prepared the cemeteries. In order to slow infection, a "mask ordinance" required all citizens—even babies—to wear gauze masks in public at all times. This rhyme was a reminder: "Obey the laws / And wear the gauze / Protect your jaws / From Septic Paws."

To meet the demand for masks, merchants offered several fashion options. There was the classic hospital-style mask (a half yard of gauze folded over like a tri-angular bandage), a more comfortable extended-muzzle version that gave the wearer a piglike appearance, or a veil that hung loose below the chin. All would prove essentially useless: in homes, where people congregated closely, masks were not required; they could also remove them to eat. Moreover, as the flu virus was as yet undiscovered, no one understood that millions of the tiny pathogens could slip through a single hole in the coarsely woven gauze. People died at about the same rate in San Francisco as in other cities. City services were unable to cope. Still, it must have been a surreal sight: thirty thousand masked San Franciscans singing, dancing, and waving flags in the Civic Center on November 11 to celebrate the armistice that marked the end of the war.

## Losers and winners

The flu had numerous repercussions. Many people who caught the flu and survived later developed *encephalitis lethargica*, an illness that caused victims to fall into an around-the-clock sleep punctuated by comas. About five million people died from this ailment before it disappeared in 1928. Those who survived never fully recovered—they were aware of their surroundings but unable to move.

In Europe, during the postwar peace negotiations at Versailles, President Woodrow Wilson caught the flu. At the time he was the most popular leader in the world: American troops had provided the needed manpower to end the war. If anyone could have rammed through an agenda, it was Wilson. Indeed, he had come to the conference to push his Fourteen Points, a plan to prevent future Great Wars. But while Wilson was too sick and weak to have much influence, the other Allies forced unpayable reparations on Germany and gained territory for themselves. In the end, the Versailles treaty was not the blueprint for a better world that Wilson had hoped for. It was "legal robbery," a treatise on revenge. Worse, the United States Senate rejected Wilson's greatest creation, a League of Nations to guarantee the peace. In the years between the wars, unemployment and hyperinflation so crippled Germany that people would listen to anyone with a plan, even the hate-filled fantasies of Adolf Hitler. World War II was virtually guaranteed.

## Just the flu

*Influenza* is an Italian word meaning "influence." The name may spring from the astrological idea that the stars and planets influence humanity, including human health. It is an ancient disease that probably first evolved in birds. Today the main reservoir of the virus resides in the flocks of wild waterfowl like ducks, geese, and gulls that spread it around the world as they migrate. They ingest the virus when they eat and excrete it in their feces. It doesn't make them sick, suggesting a long relationship between parasite and host. Domestic birds like chickens, however, are not so well adapted to the virus. It kills them. Once one chicken is infected, the disease explodes through flocks, often with devastating effects. As the virus sickens the birds, their immune systems try to make antibodies to overwhelm it. Under this kind of pressure, flu viruses are unstable. Each generation is slightly different from the last. This helps the virus outmaneuver the immune systems of some hosts, which can cause a local epidemic. Every few decades, a flu virus may morph into a form to which nearly all hosts are susceptible. This causes a global pandemic. Such was the case with Spanish influenza.

How did the flu virus start infecting us? People liv-

Alexander Fleming was searching for a bacterial cause of the Spanish flu when he discovered the first antibiotic. A stray spore of a mold, Penicillium notatum, floated onto one of his petri dishes that was already infected with a culture of staphylococcus bacteria. Fleming noted that the mold produced a substance that inhibited the growth of the bacteria. He called it "penicillin."

ing in close proximity to animals have given many pathogens an opportunity to switch hosts. At some point in the past, the influenza virus jumped from birds to people, either directly or via an intermediate host. Pigs are the most probable "mixing vessel," an animal susceptible to avian viruses whose internal environment pressures the unstable flu parasite to change just enough to be able to infect us, too. One of the places where people, domestic birds, and pigs live in close proximity is rural China. It is no surprise that most of the major flu pandemics have started there. Even the 1918 Spanish flu may have had a Chinese origin: thousands of Chinese laborers were imported to Europe during World War I to dig trenches and could have carried the disease with them.

After the Spanish influenza subsided, a worldwide flu surveillance network was developed to try to head off another pandemic. Scientists in the network now monitor the nature of yearly flu outbreaks and provide this information to pharmaceutical companies so that they can develop effective vaccines. Particular attention is paid to China and Southeast Asia. Several deadly flu epidemics have been controlled this way, including the 1957 Asian flu and the 1968 Hong Kong flu. The 1991 Hong Kong bird flu and the 2004 Asian bird flu, both of which jumped to people, were stopped by slaughtering chicken flocks that might harbor the disease. Nineteen million birds were killed in Canada's Fraser Valley alone in 2004. Since 2001, the United

States Centers for Disease Control has stepped up flu surveillance with the establishment of the International Emerging Infections Program. In 2003, the group's office in Thailand was among the first to alert the world to a pandemic of a novel flulike disease, severe acute respiratory syndrome (SARS). The pandemic was controlled, in part, by unprecedented cooperation among scientists around the world, which the flu network had made possible. That cooperation will be essential in the future. Knowledgeable scientists say that with the instability of the influenza virus, it is only a matter of time—not if, but when—until another lethal Spanish-style flu emerges. Officials at the World Heath Organization estimate that when that happens, up to a billion people around the world could fall ill. Without an effective response, they suggest, 180 million people could die. Unlike in 1918, however, we know this pandemic is coming. We can prepare for the worst.

Possibly the most important outcome of the Spanish flu was its immunological aftermath: the discovery of penicillin. Flu wasn't definitively understood to be a virus until 1933. Before that, many scientists agreed with eminent German biologist Richard Friedrich Johannes Pfeiffer that flu was caused by a bacterium. In 1928, Scottish scientist Alexander Fleming was trying to isolate that bacterium, known as Pfeiffer's bacillus. While Fleming was on vacation, a spore from a neighboring lab contaminated one of his bacterial cultures with the rare mold *Penicillium notatum*. Fleming noticed that the mold released a poison that inhibited the growth of bacteria. He had stumbled across the world's first antibiotic: a substance that could kill pathogenic bacteria. He called the substance "penicillin."

Fleming didn't follow up on his discovery, but ten years later, two other British doctors, Howard Florey and Ernst Chain, tried to find out if penicillin had medical potential. When World War II created a huge need for drugs to treat wounded soldiers, these experiments were accelerated. At the time, soldiers were losing limbs and dying from even tiny wounds that festered and progressed to gangrene. Penicillin, though useless against viruses, stopped many bacterial infections with near-miraculous power. Soldiers who would have died from infection in previous wars could now return to the battlefield, giving the Allies a significant advantage over their enemies. Penicillin production was transferred to the United States and ramped up a millionfold, from petri dishes and lab trays to huge brewery vats. The strain of *Penicillium* changed, too, from the low-yield fungus in Fleming's petri dish to a more productive strain discovered on a moldy cantaloupe in Peoria, Illinois. (A mutated version of that species, *Penicillium chrysogenum*, is still used today.) By 1945, the United States was producing enough penicillin to treat a quarter million patients a month. The age of antibiotics had begun.

# Racing with the Red Queen
*How pathogens regulate life*

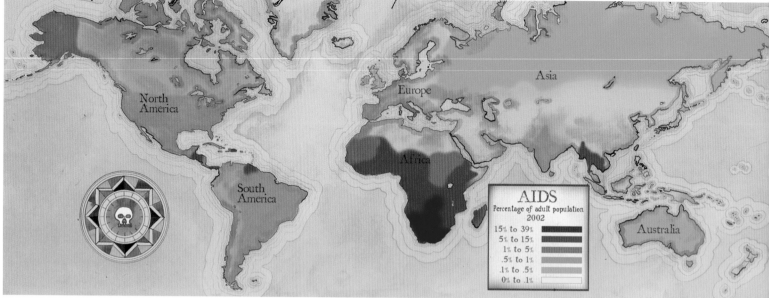

## I wish I hadn't said that

"It is time to close the door on infectious disease."

When United States surgeon general William Stewart made that pronouncement in 1967, it seemed neither hubris nor naïveté. It was a bold declaration in an age when anything seemed possible. At the time, smallpox was well on the way to being eliminated. Polio could be cured. Tuberculosis was in decline. Malaria and yellow fever were controlled. Measles was disappearing. Sexually transmitted diseases could be squelched. With infection nearly bested, chronic diseases like cancer and heart ailments seemed to be the focus of the future.

By century's end, however, nearly all of those immunological gains had been reversed. Once-proud public health care systems were faltering, victims of their own success: as fear of infectious disease faded, many governments had slashed public health funding. Parents had begun to weigh the slightly possible adverse side effects of immunizations—from autism to death—against what they perceived as the dimming chance of disease. More and more people started opting out of vaccination programs. Diphtheria, pertussis, mumps, measles, and yellow fever reemerged as health problems. Meanwhile, bacterial infections that had been disappearing at midcentury not only had returned but had proved increasingly invulnerable to antibiotics. Worried infectious-disease professionals warned that unless something

changed, even our most powerful antibiotics would eventually be useless.

As it turns out, only a single infectious genie—smallpox—has been successfully stuffed back in its bottle. By 1991, the disease disappointments of the late twentieth century would prompt weary Columbia University physician Harold Neu to this rueful wisdom: "Bacteria are cleverer than men." By 2002, Flinders University microbiology professor Peter MacDonald would make an even more sweeping admission: "Germs are smarter than people and getting smarter all the time."

Part of the problem is that since the days of Koch and Pasteur, we've thought of our relationship with disease as a kind of war. In the bloody twentieth century, where war was ubiquitous, disease was yet another enemy. Military terms began to define illness. Today the metaphors are pervasive: the human body is a fortress; microbes are the enemy; medicine is our weapon. In a time when everyone "fights" a cold, it's hard to think of infectious disease any other way. The problem with this kind of thinking is that it suggests that in disease, as in war, we can beat microbes and they'll stay beaten. Problem is, no one told the microbes.

## Paging Doctor Told-you-so

In hindsight, our current dilemma could have been predicted. As we have seen before, antibiotics don't kill off all microbes, just the weak ones. A few resistant microbes survive, reproduce, and become dominant.

Our relationship with pathogens is a never-ending competition. As we develop new measures to keep pathogens at bay, they evolve countermeasures to outwit us. So far, germs have proven smarter.

This is evolution, the force that is the real "invisible hand" pushing variation among and between all living things. Human beings, like microbes, have been pressured to change by evolution. We have evolved skin to keep microbes out, an elaborate internal immune system to neutralize those that get in, and sexual reproduction to shuffle our descendants' genetic makeup, rendering them less vulnerable hosts. For both people and microbes, the process of change occurs over thousands of generations. The difference is that microbes reproduce in hours, not years. In an evolutionary race, they always win.

To improve our odds, we've added antibacterials, antivirals, antibiotics, and other medicines to our evolutionary armamentarium. But as early as 1946, only three years after the first use of penicillin, staphylococcus bacteria began showing resistance. With the mass deployment of the drug worldwide to treat a variety of infections, resistance increased. By 1952, three-fifths of all staph infections were resistant to penicillin. Today the figure is 95 percent.

In October 1943, a second antibiotic was discovered. It was called streptomycin, and it proved to be a total cure for tuberculosis. Soon the new drug was being sold by the ton around the world; by 1955, microbes began showing resistance. With the initial success of penicillin and streptomycin, drug companies began testing soil samples from all over the world to find new antibiotic-producing bacteria and fungi to replace them. Ultimately some eight thousand antibiotics were described, a fraction of which were safe enough to be used on people. Once a commercially useful antibiotic was isolated, it was mass-produced and deployed.

In every case, bacteria adapted and became resistant. Methicillin was deployed in 1960 to treat penicillin-resistant infections. Resistance showed up the following year. Vancomycin, a powerful, expensive antibiotic, was first deployed in 1956, and by the 1960s it was being used to treat methicillin-resistant staph. By 1986, some microbes actually thrived in the poison. Resistance to vancomycin's replacement, linezolid, started showing up in 1999.

Today more than a hundred thousand tons of antibiotics are produced worldwide with annual sales of almost $5 billion. With so many pharmaceuticals flooding the environment, antibiotics have become a global evolutionary force. Hospitals, where bacteria and viruses have multiple opportunities to swap useful traits, have become centers of bacterial resistance and disease amplification. Each year millions of patients contract *nosocomial* (hospital-acquired) infections. Tens of thousands die. This is true in industrialized countries like the United States, where budget cuts have compromised basic hygiene procedures like sterilizing hospital laundry and isolating infectious individuals. It is also the case in Russia and Africa, where hospital poverty means vaccination syringes have to be reused hundreds of times, in effect injecting diseases from one patient into many others.

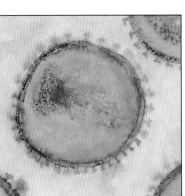

*The human immunodeficiency virus*

Bad as this is, it gets worse: some scientists are *deliberately* accelerating microbial evolution in novel directions. Around the world, military bioweapons laboratories are trying to create new pathogens with the characteristics of several different microbes (imagine plague, smallpox, and cholera deployed in a single organism). These perverse "chimeras" are engineered to overwhelm both human resistance and antibiotics. Released into the environment, either accidentally or on purpose, such pathogens could kill us all.

For a graphic reminder of what the world might be like were we to return to an age without modern hygiene and antibiotics, we have the example of the horrific Asian tsunami that occurred on December 26, 2004. In a few moments, a series of huge earthquake-generated waves killed over 150,000 people living around the Indian Ocean rim. In the days, weeks, and months that followed the disaster, thousands of injured survivors had no access to simple first aid: clean water, soap, bandages, and antibiotics. Simple wounds that could usually be treated with a twenty-five-cent pill became gangrenous. With no alternative, doctors had to do as they did during the American Civil War: cut off the dying limb to save the patient. In Indonesia, a month after the tsunami, doctors were performing so many amputations they started to run out of usable surgical saws.

## Just getting started

Viruses can evolve even more quickly than bacteria. The story of HIV, the human immunodeficiency virus, is well known. HIV is the virus that causes acquired immune deficiency syndrome (AIDS).

AIDS destroys the body's immune system, opening the door for infection by other parasites, like tuberculosis (AIDS has been instrumental in accelerating the current TB epidemic). Currently about forty million people are infected with the virus. About four million new cases occur each year, and the rate is accelerating. Since 1981, when AIDS was identified, twenty million people have died of the disease.

HIV probably jumped to us from primates, most likely in Africa, where it is now a leading cause of death. The disease is transmitted from person to person by the exchange of bodily fluids. HIV evolves so rapidly that one person may host thousands of different HIV variants. Resistance to a single drug treatment evolves not in years or months but in days. There's no cure, but HIV evolution can be temporarily arrested with an arduous, unpleasant "triple-drug cocktail." It has to be taken several times a day, every day, for the rest of an infected person's life. At current prices, it costs over $18,000 per patient per year. Recently, a variant of the virus was discovered that is immune even to this extreme treatment.

As with other plagues, AIDS has evoked the usual dismal catalog of human responses: fear, greed, humiliation, anger, blame, hate, and violence. But this unhappy record has been balanced by reason, compassion, and astonishing scientific effort. We now know the cause of AIDS, we know how to prevent it, and we know how to treat it. We don't know whether this knowledge will be enough to stop the epidemic, nor can we predict the long-term effects it will have on our social relations, political choices, and economic development. It is clear, however, that human beings need not die helplessly from AIDS. That they continue to do so is a measure of how little we have really changed since the age of the Black Death.

## Scrub-a-dub-dub

As the example of AIDS shows, racing to keep up with all this human-generated evolution is expensive—by some estimates more than $100 billion per year in the United States alone. More importantly, as the cost of treating resistant microbes rises, more and more people cannot afford the drugs. In impoverished Haiti, that includes virtually everyone except a tiny elite. In the United States, where over forty-two million people do not have health insurance, that's nearly a fifth of the population.

Is there an alternative? Of course. Resistance is a useful trait, but it exacts a cost. Remove evolutionary

*Many pathogens can modify our behavior. Toxoplasma gondii changes people's personalities and slows their reactions, making their driving more dangerous for everyone. The parasite infects half the world's human population. We get it from infected food and used kitty litter.*

pressures like antibiotics and pesticides, and resistant microbes lose their advantage over their less hardy relatives. Resistance fades. The catch is, we've gotten complacent. We need to change our behavior. Outdoors, this means a return to disciplined mosquito control, removing stagnant water sources where the insect vectors for yellow fever, West Nile virus, and malaria can breed. In hospitals, this means a return to more basic hygiene: rigorous sterilization and plain old Semmelweis hand washing. Astoundingly, American doctors comply with rigorous hand-washing procedures only 40 to 60 percent of the time. The supposedly squeaky-clean Swiss are just as bad.

Poor hand-washing habits among the general population (that means you) are responsible for the spread of many microbes, including *Toxoplasma gondii*, a protozoan that infects half the world's human population (in some places over 80 percent) with results we are only beginning to understand. Toxoplasma lives in the soil and in many kinds of mammals, especially cats. We usually become infected with toxoplasma when we change kitty litter and don't stop to clean our hands. Contaminated meat is another route. Toxoplasma is dangerous for pregnant women: it can damage the fetus. It's also bad for AIDS patients, in whom toxoplasma can cause dementia. Most people, however, are utterly unaware they host the parasite, even though it has subtle effects on personality and responses to stimuli. People infected with toxoplasma have more sluggish reaction times than the uninfected. Consequently, they are twice as likely to be involved in a traffic accident.

## End of the line

Agriculture can also play a role in slowing microbial evolution. Industrial farming relies on precisely applied fertilizers, poisons, and drugs to keep high-density monocultures of animals and plants disease-free. Some cattle ranchers and chicken farmers are experimenting with a low-tech alternative. They have switched back to old-fashioned free-range grazing and organic feed. Although herds and flocks are smaller, the need for antibiotics and chemicals is less. Ditto for potato farmers. Most American potato farms now grow Russett Burbanks, the raw ingredient for McDonald's fries. The only way to keep at bay the pests and blights that specialize in this potato variety is to drench the crop in deadly pesticides, herbicides, and fungicides. The ancient Inca method—a mix of many different organically raised potatoes—uses no expensive poisons, so farming costs are lower. In the end, fewer microbes are pressured to evolve. The food sells for more. Profits are higher. Everyone wins—except, of course, the folks selling chemicals and antibiotics.

In a few cases, some microbes may actually be eradicated, bringing their evolution to a dead stop. Through the vaccination efforts of the World Health Organization, by 2004 polio was nearly wiped out, confined to a small part of Africa. A few officials there stopped cooperating, however, and polio has once again begun to spread to other continents. If governments can cooperate, it may disappear. River blindness, another mostly African disease, is a happier tale. It may vanish due to the "strategic philanthropy" of pharmaceutical giant Merck. Free annual treatments with the company's drug Ivermectin (developed for canine heartworms) paralyze the microscopic worms that cause the disease. They can neither move nor reproduce. If all goes well, in about a decade the parasite will be extinct. The benefit to Merck? Good works, of course, but also good public relations. Such positive image building helps offset negative publicity, like the bad ink that accompanied the 2004 recall of Merck's controversial painkiller Vioxx.

## It's the poverty, stupid

Such efforts will come to naught without addressing the elephant in our collective living room: unequal access to health care among rich and poor. Global

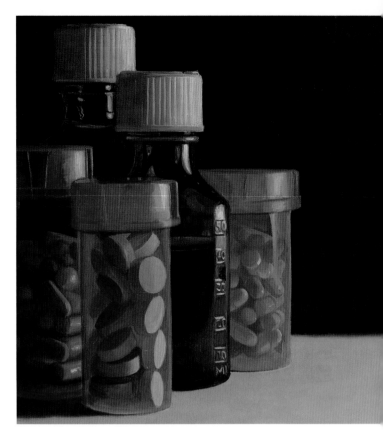

wealth has reached unprecedented concentrations. The net worth of the world's 350 top billionaires exceeds that of the bottom two and a half *billion* people. The best medical care is lavished on the rich. Pharmaceutical companies cater to them. The poor get the crumbs. Problem is, the poor are the ones with the most serious medical problems. Most of the millions of people dying from TB, cholera, yellow fever, malaria, dengue, AIDS, and other epidemic illnesses are poor. Because those at the bottom can only afford a portion of the needed drugs (or bogus drugs, or expired drugs, or the wrong drugs), they help spread multiple-drug resistance. While this "epidemiological divide" remains, quickened microbial evolution will eventually negate all the advances of the last century. Even unlimited wealth can't stop a microbe that is resistant to everything.

In countries where multi-drug-resistant microbes are prevalent, a tuberculosis treatment idea called DOTS-Plus offers a template to slow microbial evolution and save lives. DOTS (which stands for "directly observed therapy, short course") was an aggressive tuberculosis treatment strategy pioneered in New York during the 1990s after the onset of the current epidemic. DOTS requires public health workers to find TB patients wherever they are and watch them take their meds, time after time, pill after pill, until a six-month regimen is completed. It works, and the DOTS model has now been exported around the world. But as more and more TB microbes have become resistant to several drugs, DOTS has become

less useful. A new therapy, DOTS-Plus, deploys several powerful and expensive TB drugs at once in a patient for up to two years. The therapy kills all the TB microbes, not just the weak ones.

Initially, DOTS-Plus was only available to the wealthy or the well-insured. Curing poor people with multi-drug-resistant TB was not considered "cost-effective," an idea born of lingering middle-class prejudices: the lives of the poor were too chaotic, they moved a lot, they couldn't adhere to elaborate multi-drug treatments over months and years. More importantly, they couldn't pay. But a Boston-based organization, Partners in Health, working in impoverished regions of Peru, proved that the poor are just as capable as the rich—often more capable—of following complex drug regimens. With that evidence in hand, a consortium of health organizations called the Green Light Committee pressured pharmaceutical companies to drop their prices for expensive TB drugs by up to 99 percent. DOTS-Plus is now being deployed around the globe by the World Health Organization. TB evolution has been slowed, benefiting everyone, rich and poor.

## Wealth or health

Profit is a great motivator. It drives the capitalist economy. Many of the world's medical breakthroughs have been pioneered by altruistic people with noble intentions. Many more have been made by people who wanted to get rich. There's no shame in that. The problem comes when medicine focuses so exclusively on taking care of the wealthy minority of patients who can afford the best that the majority of humanity is left out. We ignore this disparity at our peril. Pathogens are equal-opportunity infectors: they don't discriminate based on address, education, skin color, or credit limit. They exploit the inequalities we have built into our health care environment to their advantage.

When health is a public good, not a private perk, everyone is better off. Retargeting health care funds from the few to the many may be one of the most effective ways to slow microbial evolution. Some countries have already approached this goal: Sweden, Singapore, Canada, and Cuba have each tried different approaches to marrying private medicine and public health. Sweden, Singapore, and Canada are wealthy nations. Cuba is quite poor. Despite these differences, each of these countries has created a health care system with greater access to better care for more people than the United States, where health care is the most expensive in the world. As you might imagine, the health care systems in Sweden, Singapore, Canada, and Cuba have problems and critics. But the results speak for themselves, especially in rates of infant mortality, in that period at the beginning of life when immune systems are fragile and people are easy prey for lethal infectious diseases. Infant mortality in all these countries is lower, and achieved at lower cost, than in the United States. Singapore's infant mortality rate, 2.2 deaths per thousand births (about a third of the American rate), is the lowest on earth. Clearly they're doing something right.

## Run, Alice, run!

If we're really going to change the way we deal with human health, we may need to think differently about disease. It turns out that the victor-and-vanquished military metaphor is not a terribly useful way to imagine microbial parasites. A better way to understand our evolutionary relationship with microbes comes, of all places, from a classic children's story. It's called the "Red Queen hypothesis," and it goes like this: as we evolve, so do pathogens; as pathogens evolve, so do we. Medicines like antibiotics and poisons like chlorine give us temporary protection from these predators. But eventually a microbe evolves that can overcome these measures. Its descendants then put the pressure back on us. Round and round we go. Like the Red Queen Alice meets in Lewis Carroll's *Through the Looking-Glass*, we're running as fast as we can just to stay in one place.

In all likelihood, we always will.

# Glossary

*Aedes aegypti*  The mosquito vector for dengue and yellow fever

**AIDS**  Acquired immune deficiency syndrome, a progressive deterioration of the immune system caused by the HIV virus. Transmitted by the exchange of bodily fluids.

**antibiotic**  A class of medical toxins produced by a variety of fungi and bacteria that inhibit the growth of pathogenic bacteria. Ineffective against viruses.

**bacillus**  A rod-shaped bacterium

**bacterium**  Any single-celled microbe without a nucleus

**chimera**  A fabulous monster; an impossible or foolish fancy; in biology, a living structure or organism created by grafting together or recombining parts of other organisms

**cholera**  A disease caused by the waterborne pathogen *Vibrio cholerae* that leads to mild to lethal diarrhea and dehydration

**coccus**  A spherical bacterium

**dengue**  A hemorrhagic fever, transmitted by the *Aedes aegypti* mosquito. Endemic to Asia, Africa, and the Americas.

**diphtheria**  An inflammatory disease of the air passages

**encephalitis**  Inflammation of the brain

**endemic**  Specific to a region or people (as a disease)

**epidemic**  Widely prevalent (as a disease)

**fluke**  A parasitic flatworm that lives in the blood of mammals

**gangrene**  Death of the tissue in part of the body

**hemorrhagic**  Accompanied by bleeding

**hepatitis**  Inflammation of the liver

**HIV**  Human immunodeficiency virus; the cause of AIDS

**influenza**  An acute infectious viral disease of the respiratory tract

**inoculate**  To implant a virus or bacterium in the human body

**measles**  An infectious viral disease characterized by a red rash

**meningitis**  Inflammation of the lining of the brain and spinal cord

**microbe**  A microscopic organism, invisible to the eye

**mumps**  A viral disease consisting of inflammation of the salivary glands, with swelling in the neck

**nosocomial**  A type of infection that is acquired while a patient is in a hospital

**pandemic**  Prevalent in a country, continent, or the entire world (as a disease)

**pertussis**  Also known as whooping cough; an infection of the respiratory system

**phlebotomy**  Therapeutic bloodletting. In Galenic medicine, used to help rebalance the bodily "humors."

**plague**  A general term for all epidemic disease; specifically, bubonic plague, a widespread disease with a high mortality rate caused by the bacterium *Yersinia pestis*

**protozoan**  A single-celled microscopic animal

**resistance**  The ability of a creature's immune system to withstand a disease, antibiotic, pesticide, or other environmental insult

**rheumatic fever**  An inflammatory disease that may develop after an infection with streptococcus bacteria

**river blindness**  An infestation of filarial worms that causes scarring in the eyes and progressive blindness

**SARS**  Severe acute respiratory syndrome; a highly infectious flulike respiratory disorder caused by a corona virus. The vector for this illness is the civet cat.

**smallpox**  A highly infectious viral disease caused by the variola virus, characterized by painful raised bumps (pustules) that scar the skin

**spirochete**  A screw-shaped bacterium

**staphylococcus**  A perfectly spherical bacterium that clusters like grapes

**streptococcus**  A type of oblong spherical bacterium, usually linked in chains

**syphilis**  A sexually transmitted disease, caused by the spirochete *Treponema pallidum*, resulting in skin cancers, disturbances of the immune system, and ultimately infections of the bones, muscles, and brain

*Toxoplasma gondii*  A protozoan that inhabits most mammals and that in human beings causes changes in personality and behavior. Can cause brain damage in fetuses and dementia in immune-compromised hosts.

**tuberculosis**  A disease caused by *Mycobacterium tuberculosis* that can manifest in the bones, stomach, skin, and lymph system, but most often appears in the lungs; characterized by the production of round nodules called tubercles

**typhoid**  An often fatal bacterial disease characterized by intestinal ulceration and inflammation; caused by the bacterium *Salmonella typhosa*

**typhus**  An acute infectious, often fatal disease transmitted by fleas and lice, caused by *Rickettsia prowazekii*; characterized by reddish spots on the body, severe nervous symptoms, and prostration

**vaccina**  The cowpox virus, used to immunize against smallpox

**vaccine**  Modified microorganisms used for preventative inoculation

**variola**  The virus that causes smallpox

**vector**  An organism that transmits a disease

**vibrio**  A comma-shaped bacterium

**virus**  Any of a class of submicroscopic pathogens that are dependent on the host cell for growth and reproduction

**West Nile virus**  A sometimes fatal viral illness transmitted by the *Culex pipiens* mosquito

**yellow fever**  A hemorrhagic fever caused by a virus in the family Flaviviridae; transmitted by the *Aedes aegypti* mosquito. Endemic to Africa and the Americas.

*Yersinia pestis*  The bacterium that causes bubonic plague

# Sources

For further reading, books for younger readers are bulleted.

Achenbach, Joel. 2003. "Our Friend, the Plague: Can Germs Keep Us Healthy?" *National Geographic.* November. http://magma.nationalgeographic.com/ngm/0311/resources_who.html.

Barnes, David S. 1995. *The Making of a Social Disease: Tuberculosis in Nineteenth-Century France.* Berkeley: University of California Press.

Cantor, Norman F. 2002. *In the Wake of the Plague: The Black Death and the World It Made.* New York: The Free Press.

Centers for Disease Control and Prevention. 2003. "Safe Water System." www.cdc.gov/safewater.

Crosby, Alfred W. 1986. *Ecological Imperialism: The Biological Expansion of Europe, 900–1900.* Cambridge: Cambridge University Press.

———. 1989. *America's Forgotten Pandemic: The Influenza of 1918.* Cambridge: Cambridge University Press.

• Darling, Kathy. 2000. *There's a Zoo on You.* Brookfield, Conn.: Millbrook Press.

Dawkins, Richard. 1989 [1976]. *The Selfish Gene.* Oxford: Oxford University Press.

Diamond, Jared. 1997. *Guns, Germs, and Steel: The Fates of Human Societies.* New York: W. W. Norton and Company.

Duffin, Jacalyn. 1999. *History of Medicine: A Scandalously Short Introduction.* Toronto: University of Toronto Press.

Dunavan, Claire Panosian. 2003. "Just an Upset Stomach?" *Discover.* July, 28–29.

Farmer, Paul. 1999. *Infections and Inequalities: The Modern Plagues.* Berkeley: University of California Press.

———. 2003. *Pathologies of Power: Health, Human Rights, and the New War on the Poor.* Berkeley: University of California Press.

• Farrell, Jeanette. 1998. *Invisible Enemies: Stories of Infectious Disease.* New York: Farrar, Straus and Giroux.

Flegr, Jaroslav. 1994. "Influence of Chronic Toxoplasmosis on Some Human Personality Factors." www.natur.cuni.cz/~flegr/toxo94.htm.

• Frerichs, Ralph R. 2003. "John Snow." www.ph.ucla.edu/epi/snow.html.

Fukuda, Mahito. 2003. "Romantic Images of Tuberculosis: A Cultural History of a Disease." Graduate School of Languages and Cultures, Nagoya University. www.ihp.sinica.edu.tw/~medicine/conference/disease/fukuda.htm.

Gadsby, Patricia. 1999. "Fear of Flu." *Discover.* January, 82–89.

Garrett, Laurie. 1994. *The Coming Plague: Newly Emerging Diseases in a World out of Balance.* New York: Farrar, Straus and Giroux.

———. 2000. *Betrayal of Trust: The Collapse of Global Public Health.* New York: Hyperion.

• Giblin, James Cross; David Frampton (illustrator). 1995. *When Plague Strikes: The Black Death, Smallpox, AIDS.* New York: HarperCollins.

Glassner, Barry. 1999. *The Culture of Fear: Why Americans Are Afraid of the Wrong Things.* New York: Basic Books.

Hoffman, Alexander von. 1998. *The Origins of American Housing Reform.* Cambridge: Joint Center for Housing Studies, Harvard University.

• Johnson, Thomas J. 2003. "A History of Biological Warfare from 300 B.C.E. to the Present." www.aarc.org/resources/biological/history.asp.

Kidder, Tracy. 2003. *Mountains Beyond Mountains: The Quest of Dr. Paul Farmer, a Man Who Would Cure the World.* New York: Random House.

Kolata, Gina. 1999. *Flu: The Story of the Great Influenza Pandemic of 1918 and the Search for the Virus That Caused It.* New York: Farrar, Straus and Giroux.

Lappe, Marc. 1994. *Evolutionary Medicine: Rethinking the Origins of Disease.* San Francisco: Sierra Club Books.

Levenson, Jay A. (editor). 1991. *Circa 1492: Art in the Age of Exploration.* New Haven: Yale University Press.

Loewen, James W. 1995. *Lies My Teacher Told Me: Everything Your American History Textbook Got Wrong.* New York: Touchstone.

Longmate, Norman. 1966. *King Cholera.* London: Hamish Hamilton.

Mann, Charles C. 2002. "1491." *Atlantic Monthly.* March, 41–53.

McNeill, William H. 1974. *Plagues and Peoples.* Garden City, N.Y.: Anchor Press/Doubleday.

Oaks, Stanley C., Violaine S. Mitchell, Greg W. Pearson, and Charles C. J. Carpenter (editors). 1991. *Malaria: Obstacles and Opportunities.* Washington, D.C.: National Academies Press.

Palumbi, Stephen R. 2001. "Humans as the World's Greatest Evolutionary Force." *Science.* September 7, 1786–90.

Porter, Roy. 2004. *Flesh in the Age of Reason: The Modern Foundations of Body and Soul.* New York: W. W. Norton and Company.

Rappuoli, Rino, Henry I. Miller, and Stanley Falkow. 2002. "The Intangible Value of Vaccination." *Science.* August 7, 937–41.

Rock, Andrea. 2004. "Toxic Tipping Point." *Mother Jones.* March/April, 68–77.

Rose, Mark. 1996. "Yaws Origin." *Archaeology* 49, 3. www.archaeology.org/9605/newsbriefs/yaws.html.

———. 1997. "Origins of Syphilis." *Archaeology* 50, 1. www.archaeology.org/9701/newsbriefs/syphilis.html.

• Saghir, Tarek. 1999. "Science in Islam: Islamic Influence on the European Renaissance; Islamic Impact on Medicine." www.islamic-paths.org/Home/English/History/Science/Medicine.htm.

Sontag, Susan. 1978. *Illness as Metaphor.* New York: Farrar, Straus and Giroux.

———. 1989. *AIDS and Its Metaphors.* New York: Farrar, Straus and Giroux.

Specter, Michael. 2005. "Nature's Bioterrorist." *The New Yorker.* February 28, 50–61.

Spielman, Andrew, and Michael D'Antonio. 2001. *Mosquito: A Natural History of Our Most Persistent and Deadly Foe.* New York: Hyperion.

Terazawa, Aya, Rusli Muljono, Lisawati Susanto, Sri Margono, and Eiji Konishi. 2003. "High *Toxoplasma* Antibody Prevalence Among Inhabitants in Jakarta, Indonesia." *Journal of Infectious Disease* 56: 107–9.

Thomson, Jim. 2000. "The Haitian Revolution and the Forging of America." *The History Teacher.* November. www.historycooperative.org/journals/ht/34.1/thomson.html.

Tschanz, David W. 1999. "Typhus Fever on the Eastern Front in World War I." http://scarab.msu.montana.edu/historybug/WWI/TEF.htm.

———. 1999. "Yellow Fever and the Strategy of the Mexican-American War." http://scarab.msu.montana.edu/historybug/mexwar/mexwar.htm.

Tuchman, Barbara W. 1978. *A Distant Mirror: The Calamitous 14th Century.* New York: Alfred A. Knopf.

University of the Witwatersrand, Molecular Mycobacteriology Research Unit. 2003. "The History of Human Tuberculosis." www.wits.ac.za/myco/index.htm.

Ward, Peter. 2001. *Future Evolution: An Illuminated History of Life to Come.* New York: Times Books.

Webster, Donovan. 2000. "Malaria Kills One Child Every 30 Seconds." *Smithsonian.* September, 32–44.

Wong, George. 2003. "The Aftermath of Penicillin." www.botany.hawaii.edu/faculty/wong/BOT135/Lect23.htm.

Zimmer, Carl. 2000. *Parasite Rex: Inside the Bizarre World of Nature's Most Dangerous Creatures.* New York: The Free Press.

*For François Dubau, 1955–2004*

## Acknowledgments

*Outbreak* is a book of science and history. Any errors are my responsibility.
Still, no book is created alone. I am grateful to the many people who helped with this one. Marion Weber helped me design the handsome dummy I used to pitch this idea to Crown Books for Young Readers. The San Juan Library's interlibrary loan program was my essential research tool. Paul Chadwick provided insightful critiques of my illustrations. Trudy Loucks, couturier at San Juan Community Theatre, provided me with the props and costumes I used to make these paintings. Daniel and Judy Finn, Fred and Xiao Fei Yockers, Marsha Rachlin, Elizabeth Pratt, Randy Hill, Ben White, Tom Holzhauser, Ladd Holroy, my wife Rebecca, my daughter Wynn, and my son Parks were my gracious models.
Dr. Amy Bloom of the Bureau of Global Health, Office of HIV/AIDS, Technical Leadership and Research Division of the U.S. Agency for International Development in Washington, D.C., offered me useful research advice. Dr. Robert Quick of the Foodborne and Diarrheal Diseases Branch of the Centers for Disease Control and Prevention (CDC) in Atlanta critiqued my chapter on cholera and informed me about the CDC's Safe Water System. Dr. Susan Mahoney of Inter-Island Medical Center, San Juan Island, and Dr. Joseph Knight of Group Health, Seattle, read drafts of my manuscript. So did Sam Connery of Friday Harbor, who also supplied me with a voluminous array of articles, newspaper clippings, magazines, and books on infectious disease that were the basis for many chapters. They all provided valuable feedback. Kevin Brown, trust archivist and Alexander Fleming Laboratory Museum curator at St. Mary's Hospital in London, provided important archival references for my painting of the discoverer of penicillin.
My astute editor at Crown, Michelle Frey, ensured that my manuscript for *Outbreak* was on track, on target, and on time. Her ideas were invaluable, including the title. Alison Kolani was the eagle-eyed copy editor who helped me keep my spelling and facts straight. Jason Zamajtuk designed the crisp, clean look of the book under the gentle supervision of Isabel Warren-Lynch, Crown's art director.
Finally, *Outbreak* could not have been created without the members of my family, who were unfailingly supportive and helpful at every turn.
To all of you: thank you.

Published by Crown Publishers, an imprint of Random House Children's Books,
a division of Random House, Inc., New York.
CROWN and colophon are trademarks of Random House, Inc.
www.randomhouse.com/kids

**Library of Congress Cataloging-in-Publication Data**
Barnard, Bryn.
Outbreak : plagues that changed history / written and illustrated by Bryn Barnard.
p. cm.
ISBN 0-375-82986-5 (trade) — ISBN 0-375-92986-X (lib. bdg.)
1. Communicable diseases—History— Juvenile literature. 2. Epidemics—History—Juvenile literature.
3. Diseases and history—Juvenile literature. I. Title.
RA643.B37 2006 614.4'973—dc22 2005015086

MANUFACTURED IN CHINA
First Edition
November 2005
10 9 8 7 6 5 4 3 2 1